READING

GULLIVER

TRAVELS

INTO SEVERAL

Remote Nations

OF THE

WORLD.

IN FOUR PARTS.

By *LEMUEL GULLIVER,*
firſt a Surgeon, and then a Captain
of ſeveral S H I P S.

VOL. I.

LONDON:
Printed for Benj. Motte, *at the Middle*
Temple-Gate *in* Fleet-ſtreet.
M, DCC, XXVI.

READING

GULLIVER

Essays in celebration of JONATHAN SWIFT'S classic

Dublin City Public Libraries MMVIII

First published 2008 by
Dublin City Public Libraries
Dublin City Library and Archive
138-144 Pearse Street
Dublin 2

Text © the contributors 2008
Concept © Dublin City Public Libraries

Designed by: Bothwell & Vogel Graphic Design Consultants
Printed by: Future Print

ISBN 0-946841-92-6
ISBN 978-0-946841-92-9

Contents

Foreword

Deirdre Ellis-King *Dublin City Librarian*

Given the connection of Dean Jonathan Swift with Dublin - and his place in the literary heritage of the city - it is particularly pleasing for me to present this collection of essays on his immortal classic, *Gulliver's Travels*, specially commissioned by Dublin City Public Libraries.

First published nearly 300 years ago, in 1726, it remains one of the great satirical masterpieces of English literature. Written in the style of a contemporary travel book, *Gulliver's Travels* has appeal for readers on many levels, savagely lampooning the politics, religious bigotry and social mores of Swift's own time - and still, after so many years, having much to say about the human condition. Swift's work has also been enjoyed by generation upon generation of children as a wonderful story of adventure and fantasy, indeed there can hardly be a child who is not familiar with the image of the giant Gulliver dwarfing the little people of Lilliput.

Remarkably, it has never been out of print and is available in countless languages, reaching every part of the globe, including some of those regions purportedly visited by Captain Gulliver on his voyages.

The essays which follow offer several valuable insights to readers new and old. The first, by Ian Campbell Ross, sets the scene. He explores Dublin as it was in Swift's time, and the way in which the writer interacted with the city of his birth. Andrew Carpenter, in his contribution, proposes taking a copy of *Gulliver's Travels* to a desert island for sustenance in the absence of all other literary fare. Mary Shine Thompson puts herself in the shoes of John Gulliver, looking at his father's travels with some scepticism and expressing dissatisfaction with the treatment of children in the narratives. Both Valerie Coghlan and Celia Keenan examine the evocative illustrations which have accompanied various editions of the text, the first appraising early styles of illustration and the second honing in on the most recent retelling, illustrated by Chris Riddell. Máire Kennedy looks at some of the early editions of Gulliver, highlighting treasured editions to be found in the collections of Dublin City Public Libraries. Finally, Eibhlín Evans outlines the influence of Swift's humour and his approach to satire on Anglo-Irish writing. In all, we find a broad spectrum of Swiftian readers who delight in sharing a love of *Gulliver's Travels*. The colourful illustrations which accompany the text give a flavour of the diversity, ingenuity and beauty that characterise the many different artistic visions of Swift's enduring satire.

Swift Bust

I

SWIFT and Dublin

Ian Campbell Ross

As I ſtroll the city, oſt I
Spy a building large and loſty,
Not a bow-shot from the College,
Half a globe from sense and knowledge.
By the prudent architect
Placed againſt the church direct;
Making good my grandam's jeſt,
Near the church – you know the reſt.

(*A Character, Panegyric, and Description of the Legion Club*, ll. 1-8)

And Jesus asked him, What is thy name? And he said, Legion: because many devils were entered into him
(Luke. viii. 30.)

A decade after he had published *Travels through Several Remote Nations of the World*, Jonathan Swift began his last great poem much closer to home. 'The Legion Club' (1736) opens with the lines:

> As I stroll the city, oft I
> Spy a building large and lofty,
> Not a bow-shot from the College,
> Half a globe from sense and knowledge. (ll. 1-4)

In many respects, this is a remarkably confident opening to any eighteenth-century poem and even more so for a writer who, at almost seventy years of age, and increasingly infirm from a degenerative illness that had dogged him for much of his life, was close to the end of his writing career. What is especially notable about these lines, however, is less immediately apparent today, to readers familiar with, say, James Joyce's *Ulysses* (1922), Patrick Kavanagh's 'Raglan Road' (1946), or Roddy Doyle's *Barrytown Trilogy* (1987-1991). Today, Dublin is not only the setting of much modern writing, it has become – above all through Joyce's use of the city – one of the mythic locations of western literature, as the Bloomsday celebrations held on 16 June remind us annually.

It was not always so. One of the first things Swift's contemporaries would have noticed about the opening of 'The Legion Club' and one of the first things modern readers of the poem must still understand is that the city through which Swift strolls is Dublin. This simple fact is remarkable since the poem was not first published in the Irish capital but rather – and like *Gulliver's Travels* – in London.

The fact of English publication is not without reason, it must be said, since the 'The Legion Club' is a truly ferocious attack on members of the Irish parliament, whom Swift depicts as diabolic - vain, ill-qualified, self-absorbed madmen, more interested in backhanders than the public good – so that it is not surprising that the poem was not published at all in Ireland until almost twenty years after Swift's death in 1745. What is certain, however, is that Swift expected his readers to be able to recognise the city through which he makes his way as Dublin – and so to be able to pick up on the topographical references that follow: 'As I stroll the city, oft I/Spy a building tall and lofty/Not a bow-shot from the College'. The building that Swift spies as he strolls was, in fact, a new one: the modern parliament house – now the Bank of Ireland – on College Green, designed by Edward Lovett Pearce. Begun in 1729, just seven years before Swift wrote 'The Legion Club', the building was occupied by the parliament from 1731, though the colonnade was not completed until 1739; Edward Lovett Pearce was knighted there in 1732. Once we know this, then it is easy to understand the reference to the 'College' as being to Trinity College, and specifically to its West Front (this is not the present West Front, which dates only from the 1750s, but the earlier façade it replaced, built around the end of the seventeenth century).

Having in the poem's fourth line given a first, mildly satirical glance at the Irish parliament which, though 'Not a bow-shot from the College' is 'Half a globe from sense and knowledge', Swift continues with four lines that evoke the physical surroundings of the parliament's new home, in order to exploit them for further comic effect:

> By the prudent architect
> Placed against the church direct;
> Making good my grandam's jest,
> *Near the church* – you now the rest. (ll. 5-8)

The church to which Swift refers in these lines has long since disappeared but was once a notable Dublin landmark: St. Andrew's church, usually known as the 'Round Church'. The popular name was not quite accurate in fact, since the church, built in the 1660s following the Restoration of Charles II and eventually destroyed by fire in the 1860s, had been built on an elliptical plan. Swift's mention of the church, however, is intended primarily not to fix the position of the parliament house – already an imposing building well known to Dubliners, if not those beyond the Irish capital – but to facilitate a joke. The location of the parliament house next to the church is seen as 'Making good my grandam's jest,/ *Near the church* – you know the rest': an allusion to the popular proverb: 'Near the church and far from God'.

Throughout his poem, in fact, the physical fabric of Dublin figures as a symbolic location for Swift's satirical attack on Irish politicians. For a while, Swift toys with the notion of wanting to destroy the parliament, as a means of destroying those whom it contains:

> Could I from the building's top
> Hear the rattling thunder drop,
> While the devil upon the roof,
> If the devil be thunder-proof,
> Should with poker fiery red
> Crack the stones, and melt the lead;
> Drive them down on every skull,
> While the den of thieves is full. (ll. 21-28)

Parliament House 1811

Eventually, Swift decides that the building may be allowed to survive since, he suggests playfully, Lovett Pearce's work – the finest parliament building in Europe at the time – will fit in with his own plans for the city:

> Yet should Swift endow the schools
> For his lunatics and fools,
> With a rood or two of land,
> I allow the pile may stand. (ll. 35-38)

For some years previously Swift had been entertaining plans for permanently altering the physical and moral fabric of Dublin with a new building to be erected at his own expense after his death. 'The Legion Club' represents the Irish parliament as a madhouse, a bedlam, but a more compassionate Swift had long been a director of the Bethlehem (or Bedlam) hospital for the insane in London and not only had a particular interest in the treatment of the psychologically disturbed but projected a similar, but more humanely-designed, building for Dublin. Having already persuaded his friend Hester Johnson, the 'Stella' of his poems and the 'Journal to Stella', to leave a substantial bequest to another well-known charitable institution in the capital - Dr. Steevens's Hospital, of which he was a director also - Swift left money in his own will for the building of St. Patrick's Hospital, which not only survives today physically but which, greatly enlarged, is still used for the purposes Swift designed over 250 years ago.

St. Patrick's 1828

His bequest to the new hospital was the last act of Swift's life. His (often troubled) relationship with Dublin, with Ireland, had begun much earlier. Jonathan Swift was born on 30 November 1667, in Hœy's Court, near Dublin Castle; he died in the Deanery House of St. Patrick's Cathedral on 19 October 1745. So much is certain. It is certain too that during the course of a life of seventy-eight years, Swift lived for some sixty-four years in Ireland, much of that time spent in Dublin itself. Having long aspired to a more glittering career in England, Swift became Dean of St. Patrick's Cathedral in Dublin in 1713 and from the following year until his death only twice left Ireland, for short visits in 1726 and 1727. To read Swift's works in verse and prose is to become aware of the extent to which Ireland is a recurring subject and location for the author, from his earliest surviving work 'Ode: to the King, on his Irish expedition and on the success of his arms in general' (1690) to the impromptu epigram, 'Behold a proof of Irish sense!' (c. 1742/1745), composed in old age during a walk in the Phœnix Park.

Why then, we might ask, does Swift's most celebrated work, *Travels through Several Remote Nations of the World* (1726) – better known as *Gulliver's Travels* – both begin and end in London? Why should Lemuel Gulliver have lived in Redriff and not Ringsend? Why did Swift make the first of his two visits to England in the 1720s for the specific purpose of taking with him to London the manuscript of *Gulliver's Travels*, in order to arrange for its publication in the English capital? The answers to these questions must be sought both in the values of the literary culture in which Swift had been educated, and in elements of his own personal psychology.

Rocque Map 1756

Throughout much of his life, Swift showed a very real engagement with the city in which he had been born and in which he would eventually die. That engagement was both with the physical realities of contemporary Dublin and with the ways in which the capital's changing fabric might be turned into an imaginative moral landscape. As we have seen, in 'The Legion Club' Dublin becomes an emblematic space in which the attributes of a great city – understood as the location of political power, religion, learning, and art – are perverted by impotent, irreligious, ignorant, barbaric politicians, leading the writer in his gloomier moments to characterise the Irish capital as 'wretched Dublin, in miserable Ireland'.

Comparing the poetically confident opening of 'The Legion Club' with the despairing sentiments of the poem as a whole, we might find it either surprising that Swift so rarely writes of Dublin in the way he does here, or remarkable that he did so at all. Yet in representing the city he knew best in verse or prose, Swift had to confront two problems: first, how the *city* might be represented in literature and, secondly, how the particular city of *Dublin* might be represented at all.

Like all men of his time and social class – women were not accorded the same educational opportunities – Swift received a traditional humanist education, both at Kilkenny College and later at Trinity College Dublin. Such an education, in Ireland as elsewhere, was grounded in the study of the most admired writers of classical Greece and, particularly, Rome. It was from these that Swift and others of his age learned how the city and the country were to be appropriately represented in poetry and imaginative prose. The countryside came first. In Greek pastoral poetry, the countryside was a place of natural fertility and of (a sometimes fragile) harmony between the shepherds and goatherds tending their flocks, and the rest of the natural order. The leading Greek pastoral poets – Theocritus, Bion, and Moschus – lived variously in Sicily at a time (from the fourth to second centuries B. C.) when that island was culturally and linguistically part of the Greek world, and when urban settlements retained a close connection with the countryside beyond their walls.

The greatest Roman pastoral poet, Virgil - born into a rural family near
Mantua in 70 B.C. – transformed the Greek world of Theocritus and his fellow-
pastoralists into a vision of life in Roman Italy in his *Eclogues* (c. 42-37 B.C.)
and considered the art of farming in more detail in his *Georgics* (c. 37-30 B.C.),
composed as the Roman empire began to expand. Shadows pass over the rural
scene – Virgil himself lived through a period of civil war – but the poet leaves
his readers in little doubt that the best life is to be lived in the countryside.
It was a vision that held enormous appeal for readers not only in Virgil's own
day but throughout the Renaissance and up to the lifetimes of Swift and his
contemporaries. Virgil's contemporary, Horace, wrote one of the most celebrated
poems on this theme: his fourth epode, the 'Beatus ille', opening with lines that
Swift's friend, the poet Alexander Pope, would echo in 'On Solitude':

> Happy the man, whose wish and care
> A few paternal acres bound,
> Content to breathe his native air,
>   In his own ground. (ll. 1-4)

For Pope, as for other essentially middle-class poets and their readers, such
sentiments were more the stuff of wish-fulfilment than reality, least of all the
often harsh reality of actual rural existence. Even Swift was not immune from
such thoughts, however, and his imitation of Horace's *Satires*, 2.6 opens:

I often wish'd that I had clear
For life, six hundred pounds a year,
A handsome house to lodge a friend,
A river at my garden's end,
A terrace walk, and half a rood,
Of land, set out to plant a wood. (ll. 1-6)

The entire poem, in fact, depends on the implicitly understood contrast between an ideal (and idealised) rural existence and the uncertainties and fatigues of city life. Written in 1713, shortly after Swift had been made Dean of St. Patrick's Cathedral, Dublin, but while he was in England, frequenting the court and enjoying the friendship and company of leading politicians and writers, the poem concludes with Swift's professed desire to return to the simple country life of his parish in County Meath:

Thus in a sea of folly tossed,
My choicest hours of life are lost;
Yet always wishing to retreat;
Oh, could I see my country seat!
There leaning near a gentle brook,
Sleep or peruse some ancient book;
And there in sweet oblivion drown
Those cares that haunt a court and town. (*Satire* 2.6 ll. 105-12)

The rustic idyll these lines evoke was, however, very far from being the world Jonathan Swift really wished to inhabit in 1713. As ambitious as any contemporary writer, clergyman, or politician – and he was all three – Swift had little real wish to spend his time in rural obscurity, least of all in Ireland.

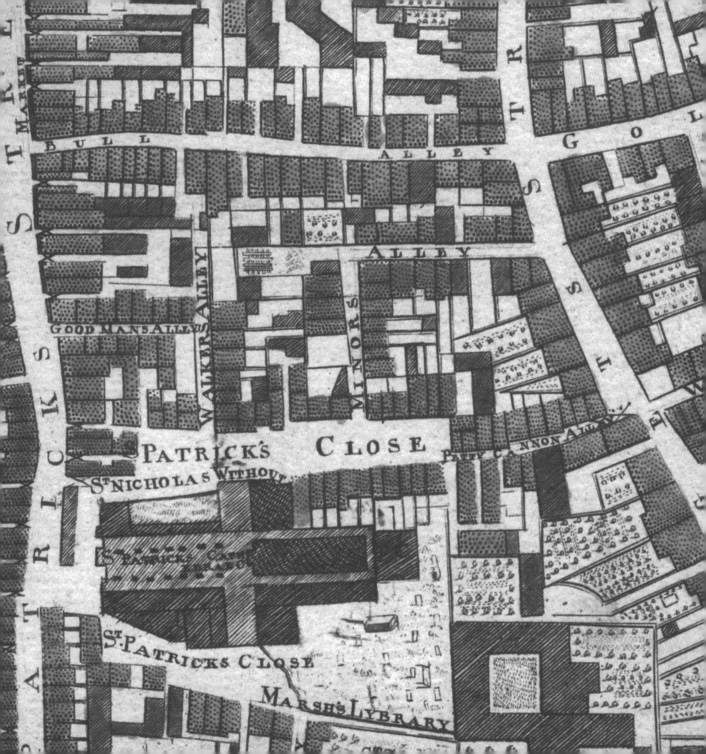

BULL ALLEY

ST MARSH

GOL ST R

ALLEY

ALLEY

MINORS

GOOD MANS ALLEY

WALKERS ALLEY

PATRICK'S CLOSE

PATTY CANNON ALLEY

ST NICHOLAS WITHOUT

ST PATRICKS CLOSE

MARSH'S LYBRARY

When he had been in Laracor a few weeks earlier, he had occupied much of his time writing to friends in London, complaining of the insufferable dullness of country life. In one letter headed simply 'The Country in Ireland', he wrote 'I am here in a way of sinking into utter oblivion' (letter of 3 August 1713), and a month later he lamented that he was now 'fitter to look after Willows, and to cutt Hedges' than play the part in national politics to which he aspired. In terms of the pœtic imagination, however, everything that Swift's culture had taught him to read and admire suggested a contrast between an urban existence that was stressful and morally corrupt and a rural life that was both peaceful and innocent.

This tension was not peculiar to Swift. His friends, Alexander Pope and John Gay, author of *The Beggar's Opera* (1728), both wrote in praise of an idealised country life, while spending as much time as possible in the city. The opening section of *The Deserted Village* (1770) is one of the most famous of all portrayals of an ideal rural community yet its author, Oliver Goldsmith, spent much of his adult life in London. In his famous imitation of Juvenal's third verse satire, *London* (1738), Samuel Johnson enquired:

> For who would leave, unbrib'd, Hibernia's land,
> Or change the rocks of Scotland for the Strand?

to which question T.S. Eliot would wittily reply 'Samuel Johnson, if anyone'.

It was, in fact, Samuel Johnson who, in very different vein, famously remarked 'When a man is tired of London, he is tired of life'. The idea of the city as a source of endless fascination as well as being the centre of all worthwhile political and cultural activity was, in effect, the obverse of the notion of the countryside as the site of the ideal existence. This idea too has its roots in classical antiquity. The speaker of the 'Beatus ille' is an inhabitant of the city of Rome whose sentiments in praise of a country life constitute the entire subject matter of Horace's poem – except for its brief closing section in which the speaker decides to leave the country be and to remain in the city after all. Augustan Rome, where Horace lived, was during the poet's lifetime the centre of a great and expanding civilisation. So too was London during the lifetime of Swift. And if much early-eighteenth century writing offers a conventionally laudatory view of the pleasures of the country, so does a great deal of contemporary and later writing insist on the attractions of London, which acted as a magnet to ambitious men (and some women) from the English provinces as well as from Scotland, Wales, and Ireland. For aspiring writers, the attractions of the metropolis were obvious, for London was increasingly the leading centre of English-language print culture. It was the Dublin-born Richard Steele, along with the English provincial Joseph Addison, who most eloquently evoked the attractions of city life, in essays in *The Tatler* (1709-10) and *The Spectator* (1711-12). Addison, in his account of twenty-four hours in London (*The Spectator*, no. 454), represents the modern city as offering an exciting new form of social experience, one running entirely counter to life in the country, since life in the now well-lit city did not come to a halt when the sun set but continued unabated around the clock.

Whatever he may have written in his classically-inspired verse, Swift was not immune to the attractions of modern city life. Spending much of the period between 1707 and 1714 in London – initially looking after the affairs of the Church of Ireland – Swift wrote to friends in Dublin of his experiences in a London that was not simply a place of business but of a world of new friends, new buildings, new books, new plays, new places to dine, new opportunities for shopping. Not everything was ideal. In comparison to the country, London was noisy, dirty, even dangerous. Despite such drawbacks, however, the novelty of the city made it a place of endless fascination.

To describe such a city, new forms of writing were required. Newspapers, periodical essays, and the emerging form of the novel all addressed the pleasures and challenges of urban life. How might the poet represent the city in ways that acknowledged its attractions? Novelty seemed the answer. And here Swift was a genuinely innovative poet. Like his well-off contemporaries, he had been educated to admire classical poetry. Could classical genres be turned to good effect in depicting the city? In two mock-pastoral poems – one imitating the eclogue, the other the georgic – Swift offered readers of, respectively, *The Tatler* and *The Spectator* parodic versions of classical poems. 'A Description of the Morning' (1709) and 'A Description of the City Shower' (1710) invert the traditional relationship between the city and the country or between the representations of these in poetry offering, for example, a vision of rain that does not refresh and renew the countryside but rather brings chaos to the city. Surveying the streets of central London after the rain, the poet describes how:

Now from all parts the swelling kennels flow,
And bear their trophies with them as they go:
Filths of all hues and odours, seem to tell
What ſtreets they sailed from, by the sight and smell.
They, as each torrent drives with rapid force
From Smithfield, or St Pulchre's shape their course;
And in huge confluent join at Snow Hill ridge,
Fall from the conduit prone to Holborn Bridge.
Sweepings from butchers' ſtalls, dung, guts, and blood,
Drowned puppies, ſtinking sprats, all drenched in mud,
Dead cats and turnip-tops come tumbling down the flood.
(*Description of a City Shower*, ll. 53-63)

As the eighteenth century went on, the city came increasingly to serve as the legitimate subject-matter in poems from Mary Wortley Montagu's *Town Eclogues*, John Gay's *Trivia; or, the Art of Walking the Streets in London* or Pope's *The Dunciad* (1728; 1744) to William Blake's coruscating 'London' (1795) or Wordsworth's admiring sonnet on London as seen from Westminster Bridge that begins: 'Earth has not anything to show more fair' ('Upon Westminster Bridge', 1802).

What all these poems have in common, of course, is that the city described is London. In the early-eighteenth century, London was the greatest of all European cities, followed by Paris, Venice, Naples, Amsterdam and Lisbon. Towards the end of Swift's lifetime, its rapidly-increasing population reached almost 700,000 – in contrast to the two next largest English cities, Bristol and Norwich, whose inhabitants numbered no more than 50,000 or so each. By these standards, Dublin – whose population of c. 45,000 in 1685 had grown to 92,000 by 1725 and would reach around 120,000 by the time of Swift's death – was large but scarcely a match for London. And, as Swift would argue in a great deal of political writing, above all in the 1720s and 30s, its political influence was small since, while Ireland might be a nation, its parliament's capacity to legislate on the country's behalf was severely limited by the provisions of Poynings' law, as strengthened by the 1720 Declaratory Act.

This is not to underestimate the importance of Dublin during the eighteenth century: it was Europe's eleventh most-populated city, after all, larger than Madrid, Milan or Berlin. Moreover, the city Swift knew in the last thirty years of his life was developing not only in population but in prosperity and in the magnificence of its buildings. Since he was a great walker, Swift came to know this city well. Even when he was an undergraduate, the main College building was a fine one, though not as imposing as the Royal Hospital at Kilmainham - designed by Sir William Robinson – which, it was suggested, might better serve as the university than as a home for old soldiers.

St. Stephen's Green was being laid out and the present plan of the city centre was taking shape, with Ormonde Quay, Capel Street, Mary Street, and Jervis Street being started and Essex Bridge built to link these with the older city south of the Liffey. Here, close to Dublin Castle, stood the Tholsel, the old corporation building that then housed the Royal Exchange. The castle itself – home to the Irish Lord Lieutenant, when in residence (which was not often) – was slowly being changed, in line with contemporary taste, away from its original medieval design. These developments had already given Dublin a more modern appearance by the end of the seventeenth century, very much at odds with what survived of the fabric of the medieval city: both Christ Church and St. Patrick's Cathedrals, for instance, had houses built right up alongside them, sharing a wall with them, in what – to modern conservationist eyes - appears to smack of randomness, if not actual vandalism.

In the opening decades of the eighteenth century, this modernisation of the city continued, and Dublin began to acquire many of the buildings that still remain today. The Mansion House in Dawson Street was built in 1710 and became the residence of the Lord Mayor five years later; the old Custom House, designed by Thomas Burgh (the predecessor of James Gandon's masterpiece on Custom House Quay) was erected close to Essex Bridge in 1707; and Burgh's Old Library of Trinity College was built over the course of two decades between 1712 and 1733 (though the barrel-vaulted ceiling was added in the late-1850s). St. Anne's church in Dawson Street, St. Werburgh's, and St. Mary's in Mary Street were all built or rebuilt during these years - as, of course, was Edward Lovett Pearce's Parliament House.

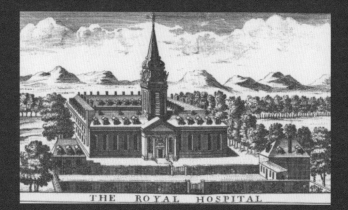

THE ROYAL HOSPITAL

FRONT OF THE COLLEDGE

The question then returns: why should Swift - who had written celebrated urban pastorals for English periodical readers; who showed himself, in the *Journal to Stella*, to be fascinated with the details of modern urban life; who, as Dean of St. Patrick's, contemplated adding a brick spire to the cathedral – have found it so hard to write about Dublin. The answer is a complex one but just as in England, there was scant tradition of imaginative writing about cities other than London, so there was little sense that Dublin might be the legitimate subject of ambitious pœtry. Like the literature of classical Rome, eighteenth-century literature in English was, above all, metropolitan in its bias. It was by the standards of the metropolis – understood as the locus and epitome of the age's cultural values – that the remainder of the world must be judged. Even in an age when landownership was the key to political and social power, those who could afford it wintered in London, at least while parliament was in session.

John Brooking

Likewise, the most affluent of Irish landowners build townhouses in the Irish capital, and Iveagh House, Tyrone House (now the Department of Education), Clanwilliam House (85 St. Stephen's Green, now part of Newman House), and Leinster House were among the magnificent private residences built in Swift's lifetime – though the Irish parliament was characteristically in session for less than six months during any two-year period.

When Swift did come to take Dublin as his subject in one of his most fascinating poems, written in the 1720s, he re-imagined the Irish capital as a second London, as contemporary poets – John Dryden or Pope, for instance – imagined London as a second Rome. In 'To Charles Ford, Esq, on his Birthday' (1723), Swift appealed to an Irish friend to return from England to Ireland. 'In London', he asks rhetorically, 'what would you do there?'. Of course, Swift knew very well what might be the attractions London held for a young, cultured Irishman. Dublin, by contrast, Swift suggests is politically and culturally nowhere. Recalling his own enforced return to the city after the death of Queen Anne in 1714 put an end to any hopes he might have had of preferment within the Church in England, Swift writes:

> I thought my very spleen would burst
> When fortune drove me hither first;
> Was full as hard to please as you,
> Nor person's names, nor places knew;
> But now I act as other folk,
> Like prisoners when their gall is broke. (ll. 51-56)

The resignation that characterises these lines, however jocular, is not a great enticement to Ford to return. And it is now that Swift changes tactic, construing Dublin as another London:

If you have London still at heart,
We'll make a small one here by art:
The difference is not much between
St. James' Park and Stephen's Green;
And Dawson Street will serve as well
To lead you hither as Pall Mall.
…

The Deanery House may well be matched
(Under correction) with the Thatched*
…

Can you on Dublin look with scorn?
Yet here were you and Ormonde born.
Oh were but you and I so wise
To look with Robin Grattan's eyes.
Robin adores that spot of earth,
That literal spot which gave him birth,
And swears Cushogue§ is to his taste,
As fine as Hampton Court at least.

* A tavern in St. James's Street, where Swift had dined when in London.
§ Swift noted this was the Irish name of Belcamp, home of his friend Robin Grattan.

In their day, the birthday verses to Charles Ford were private, not public, poetry and like 'The Legion Club' – though for different reasons – not published until after Swift's death.

When Swift wrote for immediate public consumption – as he did in *Gulliver's Travels* – it was important to address the cultural and political centre of Great Britain and Ireland – and that centre, for Swift, was London. Despite such contributions to the country's literature and political life as *The Drapier's Letters* (1724-1725) or *A Modest Proposal* (1729), Swift continued to believe Ireland to be too marginal to the concerns of the truly polite - i.e. metropolitan - audience he wished to reach when dealing with the fundamental questions of human existence. So, Swift took *Travels through Several Remote Nations* to London to be published. And Dublin has only a marginal role to play in the narrative of *Gulliver's Travels*: as Lindalino in Book III's allegorical account of the Wood's Halfpence controversy to which the *Drapier's Letters* were Swift's contribution (an account that, in any case, the publisher suppressed in the first edition as being too politically dangerous).

'To Charles Ford, Esq', however, reveals two important facts to be taken into account when considering Swift's broader relationship to the Irish capital. Like any city – like the London of *Gulliver's Travels* - Dublin is both a physical location and an idea. As such it does not only offer the writer material for representation; it is also susceptible to imaginative transformation by the writer's art. For Swift, the problem was the fact that he was in Dublin at all, in what he persisted - though not always with entire seriousness - as considering an 'exile' in the land of his birth. If London was for him the metropolis, how could Dublin, how could Ireland serve as the material for the writer ambitious of lasting fame, or of doing his country good? Such questions troubled Swift yet reluctantly - and facetiously at first – Swift came to see Dublin as a possible location for poetry.

Writing in the eighteenth century, the act of imagination that allowed Swift, in 'To Charles Ford, Esq' or 'The Legion Club' or elsewhere to make the contemporary city – rather than some timeless rural landscape – the location for poetry was perhaps as difficult, in its way, as was Joyce's transformation of Dublin into an epic world two hundred years later.

Swift was not alone among mid-eighteenth century poets in choosing to write about Ireland's capital in English verse during the eighteenth century – though he remains by far the best-known writer who did so. Thomas Newburgh penned 'The Beau Walk in St. Stephen's Green'. Lawrence Whyte wrote 'A Poetical Description of Mr. Neal's new Musick-Hall in Fishamble Street, Dublin'. Henry Jones, the so-called 'Bricklayer Poet of Drogheda', celebrated Bartholomew Mosse's foundation of the Rotunda Hospital in 'On the Hospital for Lying-in Women, erected in Dublin'. William Dunkin – a friend of Swift's, and the translator into English of Swift's Latin poem, 'Carberiæ Rupes' (1723) on Carbery Rocks, near Ross Carbery in Co. Cork – wrote 'On the New Bridge built on the Eastern Side of Dublin [i.e. Essex Bridge]'. Such verse is exceptional, though. Even poems that might seem to modern readers to be urban poems - James Ward's 'Phœnix Park' or 'The Smock Races at Finglas'; Richard Pockrich's 'The Temple-Oge Ballad'; John Winstanley's 'A Thought, in the Pleasant Grove at Cabragh', or Henry Jones's 'A Farewell to Apollo, and the Muses at Glasnevin' – actually engage with what were then rural locations quite distinct from the city itself.

Some less reverent lines – his last - were composed *extempore* when Swift, admired as the 'Hibernian Patriot' but a politically-disillusioned man, was being accompanied on a walk through the Phœnix Park during his final years. Observing the recently-built magazine fort that still exists in the Park, Swift allegedly improvised the following:

Behold! a proof of Irish sense!
Here Irish wit is seen.
When nothing's left that's worth defence,
We build a magazine.

The epigram is an economical reflection both of Swift's continuing interest
in the changing fabric of the city and of the increased political and imaginative
identification with Ireland -'*We* build a magazine' – in the final thirty years
of his life when he knew he would remain, without further preferment in the
Church, Dean of St. Patrick's for ever.

Despite the flash of humour in his epigram, reports of Swift in his final
years suggest his last walks, accompanied by a carer, would have been slow affairs,
painful in more senses than one. Better then to remember the Swift who in
'The Legion Club' appears as at once satirist and *flâneur*:

As I stroll the city oft I
Spy a building tall and lofty
Not a bow-shot from the College,
Half a globe from sense and knowledge.

In *Travels through Several Remote Nations*, Lemuel Gulliver roams the world.
In an important handful of imaginative works, Swift strolled through Dublin.
If Lilliput, Brobdingnag, Laputa, or Houyhnhnmland are more familiar
to modern day readers, then Swift's achievement of helping to place Dublin
on the literary map should not be overlooked.

Read more...

Christine Casey, *Dublin*,
New Haven and London,
Yale University Press, 2005.
Maurice Craig, *Dublin 1660–1860*,
1952; revised Harmondsworth,
Penguin, 1992.
Irvin Ehrenpreis, *Swift: the man,
his works, and the age*, 3 volumes,
London, Methuen, 1962-83.
Carole Fabricant, *Swift's
Landscape*, 1982,
(revised University of Notre
Dame Press, 1995).
Joseph McMinn, *Jonathan Swift*,
Basingstoke, Macmillan, 1990.
Joseph McMinn, *Jonathan's
Travels: Swift and Ireland*, Belfast,
Appletree Press, 1994.
Ian Campbell Ross, *Swift's Ireland*,
Dublin, Eason, 1983.

II

Some Thoughts on GULLIVER'S TRAVELS

Andrew Carpenter

J.G. Thomson

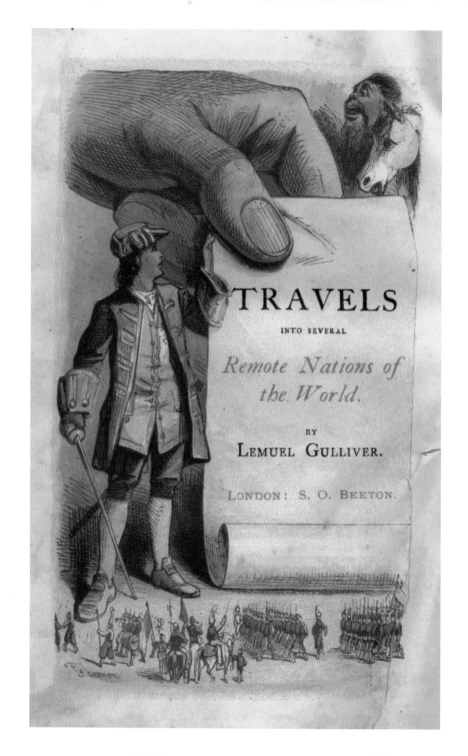

I do not know if any radio-show guest has ever selected *Gulliver's Travels* as the one book he or she would choose to take to a desert island, but it would certainly be my choice. Not only is *Gulliver's Travels* a highly entertaining tale, ideal reading-matter for those long days lying in the shade of an obliging palm-tree, but it is also a book with a serious message about human pride and self-delusion – a book which, every time I re-read it, seems to grow in significance. The proper title of the work is not *Gulliver's Travels* at all, of course, but *Travels into Several Remote Nations of the World in four parts by Lemuel Gulliver, First a Surgeon, and then a Captain of several Ships*. This full title gives us a potted biography of the supposed author and indicates that there are four separate voyages. As we leaf through the book, we find that each of the four parts has a separate map to accompany it, a map which indicates previously undiscovered lands not far from places we do know exist – Japan, for instance. And, if we should have any doubts about the authenticity of the whole work as we begin to read the text, we are likely to find that our copy contains a letter from a Richard Sympson to the reader assuring him that Lemuel Gulliver is a real man, his old and 'intimate friend': so it all seems to be genuine. And this is part of the point; the anonymous author has lured us into what seems to be a simple travel tale – which makes it all the more surprising and even shocking for us to discover that the book in our hands is not a genuine travel tale at all. In fact, as we soon discover, it is a thoroughly mixed sort of a book – part fictional adventure tale, part children's story, part morality tale, part satirical assault on man's pride, part sombre reflection of the horrors of the world. We realise we have been duped, but we continue reading our way into the text, nonetheless, gradually becoming more and more fully involved and more and more fascinated by what we read; in the end we realise that we are becoming part of the process of the book as we begin to react to Gulliver's singular views of the strange creatures he encounters and to the decidedly negative opinions these strange creatures have of him. This is a book with a 'message'; we discover that, if we are prepared to become creatively involved in the book, to respond to its outrageous exaggerations – its distorted perspectives – that very involvement will bring us beyond the book itself; it will encourage us into new ways of seeing ourselves and our own world. In effect, our experience of this book leads us to question the way we see ourselves, and we find ourselves perceiving the world and its inhabitants from at least two perspectives at once; humans are both very large and very small, very wise and very foolish. We begin to develop new (and, incidentally, profoundly 'moral') ways of interpreting human behaviour; we learn about ourselves, in fact – which is an excellent way of spending our time on the desert island.

Jonathan Swift (the man who, we now know, wrote *Gulliver's Travels*) was a troubled man, subjected, throughout his long life, to conflicting and confusing experiences. He was born in Ireland in 1667 to a Protestant English couple who had come to predominantly Catholic Ireland to make a living. Swift's father died before he was born and his nurse seems to have removed him from his mother and taken him to England for a formative period of his young life. But he then returned to Ireland and was educated at a boarding school with the sons of Anglo-Irish gentry in what was a profoundly ambiguous social, religious and political

scene. During the 1670s and 1680s – a complex and shifting time in Ireland's history – Catholics, members of the Anglican Church of Ireland, Presbyterians, native Irish, Old English and New English competed with each other for religious freedom, for political power, for the right to own Irish land or, indeed, for their very survival. By the time Swift became a student at Trinity College Dublin in his teens, confusion, double-thinking and self-deception were deeply ingrained into Irish political and religious life: towards the end of Swift's time at Trinity, the Protestant Church of Ireland and its establishment was (unenthusiastically) supporting the newly-crowned Catholic King James rather than the man who had unseated him in England, his Protestant son-in-law, William of Orange; but James, having abandoned his English throne, came to Ireland with a French/Irish Catholic army to protect his Irish throne from William, who had brought his Protestant army to the North of Ireland to drive James out of Ireland. It was a time of extreme tension, and who would be the 'real' king of Ireland – and what would be its official religion – depended simply on which side defeated the other. The decisive battle was the

Battle of the Boyne, won by William and his Protestant forces in July 1690; James and many Catholics fled to France and the Protestants took power in Ireland, not only establishing the Church of Ireland as the official church of the state but sweeping Catholics out of Parliament and off their land. The turbulence of Swift's youth was succeeded by a period of apparent calm under the rule of what became the Protestant Ascendancy. But human nature remained constant, and the people who surrounded Swift after 1690 – in Ireland or in England, where he spent much of the 1690s – were just as double-dealing, dishonest, proud, self-interested and self-deceiving as those he had known in his youth.

As Swift grew to manhood and began grooming himself to be a writer, he could see how far the actual behaviour of men and women differed from the Christian ideals to which everyone was meant to aspire; it was this sense of double values and of man's refusal to recognise the extent of his self-deception that was to influence all his work, including *Gulliver's Travels*. Swift himself was a Christian – indeed, he became an ordained minister of the Church of Ireland in the 1690s –

and so was forced to confront a great and irresolvable paradox: within all human beings is a spark (sometimes only a spark, sometimes a spark kindled to a flame) of generosity and goodness which should encourage everyone to live a life of brotherly love, tolerance and forgiveness; people seeking to live in this way fill their lives with the rhetoric of the Christian way of life. On the other hand, the same human beings can, in a moment, justify the most appalling cruelty and rapacity, twisting the rhetoric of their old position to suit the new. Even the Christian churches themselves, the Catholic, Protestant Episcopalian and Presbyterian sects, had (in Swift's eyes) perverted the message of love passed by God to mankind, and become rapacious, self-interested and self-deceiving. Equally, good and honourable intentions in other areas – in learning, in the dissemination of ideas and cultures, in the development of a fair and just society – these too had been twisted by the subtle use of rhetoric until what was said and done was almost the opposite of what it claimed to be. Words can not only be the medium for the transmission of 'right' ideas but, twisted and distorted, can drag the unsuspecting into a world of distortion and madness.

Awareness of this paradox was at the heart of Swift's mission as a writer. The manipulation of words became his obsession and the deliberate warping of meaning – often by putting words into the mouths of imaginary speakers whose vision of the world was seriously distorted – at the centre of his project: for Swift was writing not for the ordinary reader but for the man or woman 'of wit and learning' who could discern what he was doing and learn from it. However, Swift was realist enough to know that, though some readers would recognise his project and reject the visions presented to them by his mad mouthpieces – by Gulliver, by the Modest Proposer, or by the hack author of *A Tale of a Tub* – few (if any) would change their lives because of what they had read. He wrote, wryly, to his friend Alexander Pope that he hoped his Travels (i.e. *Gulliver's Travels*) would 'wonderfully mend the world'; yet the very articulation of that hope shows that he recognised that most readers would enjoy the book for its surface delights; some might be able to interpret his satirical vision but few would allow their perceptions of the world to be

changed – 'wonderfully mended' – by their experience of the book.

It is true, however, that whether they get Swift's message or not, readers invariably find *Gulliver's Travels* highly entertaining. From the moment it first appeared in London in 1726, the book has been extraordinarily popular – praised by writers, wits and philosophers from Swift's day to ours, and loved by children of all ages. Swift's spirited inventiveness gives the work an infectious freshness, and his love of absurdity keeps the reader constantly engaged; the close reader will be fascinated by the ingenuity of Swift's writing and even the more relaxed reader will still find the satiric undercurrent constantly stimulating. It is a shock to be presented with the world we recognise through the perspective glasses and the language of a Captain Gulliver who is clearly deranged – defending himself against imputations of sexual misconduct with a Lilliputian, living in a stable with his horses. And yet, Swift has lured us into thinking that Gulliver is a reliable narrator, so if we are to survive as rational or even as intelligent readers, we must become creative in our response to the text, measuring our world against the

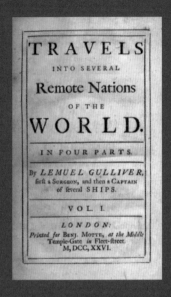

vision of the mad Gulliver, and against that of the Lilliputians, the Brobdingnagians, the Yahoos and the Houyhnhnms. We must be able to grasp the nettle of Swift's satiric message and decide how we, ourselves, wish to react to the bleak description of humanity articulated by that 'Prince of excellent understanding', the King of Brobdingnag, when he told earnest, enthusiastic Gulliver who had just spent several days extolling the virtues of human society: "I cannot but conclude the Bulk of your Natives to be the most pernicious race of little odious vermin that Nature ever suffered to crawl upon the surface of the earth."

This bleak vision of actual human behaviour came from the pen of a man who was into middle age when he started writing it. His life to this point had been full of difficulties and vexations – personal, political, professional; he has been crossed in love, frustrated in his career as a churchman, deceived and abused by politicians. Though he had risen to fame in London during the years 1700-1713 and had been called upon by highly-placed politicians to use his pen in their defence, his friends had fallen from power and he had been forced to retire from an exciting

Swift Portrait

life close to the centre of court and city life in London to the provincial world of Dublin, rewarded not with the English bishopric he so earnestly desired but with the much less glamorous position of Dean of St. Patrick's Cathedral, Dublin. Instead of enjoying scintillating London society, Swift suddenly found himself, at the age of 46, back in Ireland, a place he considered an intellectual backwater; he was forced to create company for himself and to spend time with clergymen, schoolmasters and tradesmen's wives rather than with duchesses and Privy Councillors. But within a few years, this restless man overcame the depression which initially afflicted him and found an outlet for his literary energy by writing pamphlets attacking the way Ireland was governed by the English-appointed administration and by its own Parliament. These pamphlets (the most famous of which were *The Drapier's Letters*) were remarkably successful; they wounded the government and endeared him to the people of Ireland. He became known as the Irish 'patriot' and was soon a revered and respected figure in Ireland, welcomed home from England in 1727 by cheering crowds as bonfires blazed on every street.

It seems that Swift began working seriously on his 'Travels' early in the 1720s, writing at least some of the text while staying with friends in the Irish countryside. He had always been a voracious reader, fond (among other things) of books of travel and history. We do not know how or when the basic idea for *Gulliver's Travels* came to him, though we do know that he was at work on the book by 1721 when he told his friend Charles Ford that he was 'writing a History of my Travells, which will be a large Volume and gives Account of Countryes hitherto unknown'; some critics believe the idea first came to him when he was still in London long before this. But once Swift had created a voice for Gulliver and hit upon the idea of changing viewpoints by changing Gulliver's size in the first two books of the work, he had found the ideal recipe for a powerful satire on the human condition, wrapped in an entertaining travelogue: in this format, the creatures Gulliver encountered in the four books of the work could describe his behaviour (and therefore that of all humans) objectively – without sympathy or understanding of the human predicament – while Gulliver himself could prove the stupidity of human optimism as he described the obviously absurd behaviour of the creatures he encountered as ideal. In other words, perceptions would be distorted and the language of those distortions would be so exaggerated that any sane reader would recognise the descriptions for what they were – the ranting of a madman or the words of monsters. But the language would seem (most of the time) to be sane and calm; it would be up to the reader to detect the madness of the visions presented and, as he saw them for what they were, to reject them, to turn away from them. The technique was simple enough; Gulliver would travel to lands whose inhabitants would describe him (and therefore human behaviour) without any of the comfortable self-deceptions with which men usually surround themselves. Their descriptions of him would show up not only his failings (and by extension those of other human beings) but also how easily we tell lies to ourselves about ourselves – how easily we deceive ourselves. It would be up to the reader to see and interpret this; so *Gulliver's Travels* would have a purpose not unlike that of a sermon – a session in which the reader or listener is brought face to face with his failings and, by implication at least, invited to address his own dishonesty about himself. This would be done in a work which was apparently a straightforward travel narrative. The reader would thus be lured into the work and, once there, would find himself face to face with descriptions of human behaviour based on distortions and shifts in perspective; this should force him towards a position in which he might start trying to amend himself.

One of the first indications that *Gulliver's Travels* is not what it purports to be is its physical appearance. The first edition does not look like a conventional early eighteenth-century travel book at all; whereas these were often issued in small octavo, *Travels into Several Remote Nations of the World* is in large octavo, in two substantial calf-bound volumes, well printed on good paper with maps at the beginning of each of the four voyages and a handsome engraved portrait of the supposed author as a frontispiece to the first volume. The printer was Benjamin Motte of London – a printer who had succeeded one whom Swift had used when he lived in London. Swift went to great lengths to protect the anonymity of his authorship and arranged for the manuscript (which had been copied out in a feigned hand) to be delivered to Motte in instalments by someone quite unknown to either of them. But, whether he knew the identity of the author or not, Motte recognised that the book would sell well and paid the £200 asked by the intermediary – a sum which he was told would be given to 'poor seamen'. The book appeared on 28 October 1726 and was an immediate success, the whole of the first printing being sold in a week. Almost immediately afterwards the text appeared serially in *The Penny London Post* and in an abbreviated form for children within a year. The book has never been out of print from that day to this and has been translated into scores of languages.

The immediate popularity of the book was the talk of London (and soon of Dublin too). The publisher of the *Penny London Post* asserted that the travels 'bore [a] considerable... Share in almost every Conversation both in Town and Country, not only from the Reputation of their suppos'd author, but the vast variety of wit and Pleasantry with which the several

Relations are interpos'd...'. It is said that Swift himself was delighted to hear one Irish bishop tell another that he 'did not believe a word of it'.

Because of the mysterious way in which the transcript of *Gulliver's Travels* had been delivered to the printer, and because the publisher himself had decided to make some excisions from the text for reasons of political expediency, Swift complained that Motte's text was not an accurate one. He persuaded his friend Charles Ford to make a list of all the supposed 'errors' in Motte's edition, a list which survives in an interleaved copy of that edition now in the Victoria and Albert Museum in London. However, we now have what might be termed the definitive text as Swift himself was able to oversee the next major edition of the work which was printed in Dublin in 1735.

In the years between the two main editions of *Gulliver's Travels*, Swift remained in Ireland, the centre of a circle of admiring poets – many of them attractive younger married women – and increasingly enjoying life in the city. His most famous Irish pamphlet, *A Modest Proposal*, appeared in 1729 and, though his close friend Esther Johnson ("Stella") died, he continued writing verse, much of it in tandem with his friends. His fame continued to grow and, in the mid-1730s, the Dublin printer, George Faulkner, persuaded him to oversee a new, four-volume edition of his works, to be published in Dublin. When this work appeared in 1735, it was clear that Swift himself had overseen it and the text of Faulkner's 1735 printing is the one normally used today. Over the years, Faulkner made a fortune from his many printings of Swift's works.

Satire works on the reader because the world it pictures is so exaggerated and absurd that, though he recognises elements of his own world in it, the reader finds himself laughing at the absurdities of the satiric vision. We laugh when we see the tiny Gulliver acting the fool for the enormous, Brobdingnagian farmer who 'owns' him, but we are also aware of the cruelty of the farmer in almost working Gulliver to death for his own profit. Swift would expect our laugh at the scene to be an uncomfortable one since it should alert us not only to the existence of human cruelty in our own world but to the fact that we can so easily deceive ourselves into thinking that others' cruelty has nothing to do with us. My reading

of *Gulliver's Travels* suggests otherwise – that we are all tainted by human cruelty wherever and whenever it occurs, and that we owe it to ourselves to try and prevent it whenever we can. Equally, we may laugh at the petty political chicanery of the Lilliputian court but the behaviour of the courtiers is uncomfortably similar to that of politicians in our own world. Or again, we may find the behaviour of the King of Traldragdubb (forcing those who approach him to lick the floor as they approach his throne) absurd until we read of some of the excesses of our own world. In each case, though the reader recognises the exaggeration (and laughs at it), his eyes are opened to the absurdities that pride and love of power bring to our own society and civilisation.

It is in the last part of *Gulliver's Travels*, the book in which Gulliver visits the land of the Houyhnhnms, that Swift's satire on human failings is most wounding. The horse-like Houyhnhnms, governed by reason rather than by brute emotions, see no difference between Gulliver (our human representative) and the detestable Yahoos whom they treat as slaves. As they see it, Gulliver looks like, sounds like, smells like and behaves like a yahoo –

P. J. Lynch

A VOYAGE TO BROBDINGNAG

a rather sophisticated and intelligent one perhaps, but still a yahoo. He himself, though shocked to find out how the horses categorise him, is also irrationally enthusiastic about the lifestyle of the reasonable Houyhnhnms – treating his 'master' Houyhnhnm with cringing deference and, in the end, using the word 'yahoo' to describe, without discrimination, his fellow humans. Towards the end of the book, Gulliver muses that, when he thinks of his own family, friends and countrymen or of the human race in general, he 'considered them as... Yahoos in shape and Disposition... making no other use of Reason than to improve and multiply... Vices...'. This is a bleak view of humanity – one which has been misinterpreted by critics over the years, driving them to accuse Swift of misogyny or hatred of the human race.

But this misogyny is not that of Swift himself; the speaker is his invented character, Lemuel Gulliver, a gullible and in many ways a deranged representative of the human race whose views we should recognise as unreliable and 'unsafe' – distorted as they are by the satirist to provoke our outrage (and, perhaps, as we look at our own world, to provoke our

shame). The nineteenth-century critics who damned Swift as a hater of humankind simply misread the passages in which Gulliver likens us to yahoos, mistaking the deliberate exaggerations Swift puts into Gulliver's mouth for his own views.

The key to *Gulliver's Travels* is an understanding that Swift's purpose is satiric, not vituperative. Swift certainly believed that humans behave in ways that are morally disgraceful and that they need to be alerted to this so that they can reform, but he wanted his readers to interpret the various judgements of human behaviour in the book as all, in one way or another, the results of distorted perception. Though we may agree with the King of Brobdingnag that many human beings are, indeed, 'little odious vermin', we must remember that his judgement is the product of his way of seeing – for him, humans are a mere six inches high – and of what he has been told of human activity by the absurd little Gulliver. As the king understands things, so he describes them, and Swift manipulates the king's language to shock us into recognising that there is at least some truth in what he says, given Gulliver's description of our world.

We should be ashamed at aspects of human behaviour, but not feel bound to agree with the king's judgment uncritically. For real human beings on our earth are (as we know) perfectly capable of goodness and honesty – of trying to live up to the Christian ideal: it is just that we seldom succeed in doing so.

Towards the very end of *Gulliver's Travels*, Swift drops his mask and tells us what his ideal reader of taste and discernment would have seen all along: though Gulliver is still the ostensible mouthpiece, Swift is here speaking to the reader directly; Gulliver would not find it so hard to reconcile himself to humanity (particularly to Englishmen), he says, if humans were only content with the vices and follies 'which Nature hath entitled them to.' He goes on: 'I am not in the least provoked at the sight of a Lawyer, a Pick-Pocket, a Colonel, a Fool, a Lord, a Gamester, a Politician, a Whoremonger, a Physician, an Evidence, a Subborner, an Attorney, a Traytor, or the like: But when I behold a Lump of Deformity and Diseases both in Body and Mind smitten with Pride, it immediately breaks all the measures of my Patience.'

And this is what *Gulliver's Travels* is about – human pride. This is a book with a moral message, one which aims to make the reader aware of the dire consequences which await those who succumb to the human failing that Swift's friend, Alexander Pope, described as 'the never-failing vice of fools'. For the enlightened men and women of Swift's age, and particularly for those who espoused the Christian creed, pride was the most inexplicable, the most heinous sin of all. *Gulliver's Travels* shows the reader, in comic exaggeration, the awful effects of human pride. Surely, as we lie on our desert island reading and re-reading this entertaining and challenging book, it is impossible not to take to heart its final sentence: 'I here intreat those who have any Tincture of this absurd Vice, that they will not presume to appear in my sight.'

Read more...

The standard editions are
as follows:
The Prose Works of Jonathan Swift,
edited by Herbert Davis et al.,
16 volumes, Oxford, Blackwell,
1939-68.
*The Complete Poems of Jonathan
Swift*, edited by Pat Rogers,
Harmondsworth, [Penguin], 1983.
*The Correspondence of Jonathan
Swift*, edited by Harold Williams,
5 volumes, Oxford, Clarendon
Press, 1963-72.

One of the most distinctive
editions of *Gulliver's Travels*
currently in print is that in the
St Martin's Press 'Case Studies
in Contemporary Criticism'
series: the volume is edited by
Professor Chris Fox and contains
critical essays which approach
the text from different theoretical
perspectives: Jonathan Swift,
Gulliver's Travels, edited
by Christopher Fox, New York,
[St Martin's Press], 1995.

The standard life is: Irvin
Ehrenpreis, *Swift: the man, his works
and the age*, 3 volumes, London,
Methuen, 1962-83.

Those interested in Swift's
sources and reading should
consult: Dirk F. Passmann
and Heinz J. Vienken,
*The Library and Reading of
Jonathan Swift: a bio-bibliographical
handbook*, 4 volumes, Frankfurt,
Peter Lang, 2003.

There are many excellent
critical studies on Swift
and his works: Irish readers
may find the following three
works of particular interest:
Carole Fabricant, *Swift's
Landscape*, Baltimore, 1982,
(revised University of Notre
Dame Press, 1995).
Robert Mahony, *Jonathan Swift:
the Irish identity*, New Haven
and London, Yale University
Press, 1995.
Jonathan Swift and Thomas
Sheridan, *The Intelligencer*, edited
by James Woolley, Oxford,
Clarendon Press, 1992.

III

LEMUEL GULLIVER'S Children

Mary Shine Thompson

Anonymous illustrator [1890s]

Scholars were taken utterly by surprise in 2005 to discover that John Gulliver, son of the Lemuel Gulliver whose fame rests on his fantastic voyages, had recorded an account, however tantalisingly brief, of his childhood. Dated 1760, this highly personal and frank testimony was written in his careful, copperplate hand and was discovered inserted between the leaves of a first edition of Gulliver's Travels in the basement of a house in Rotherhithe, Southwark, South London. It is likely that John Gulliver (if it is indeed he who wrote the account that follows – not all scholars are convinced of the authenticity of the account) was in his early sixties when he committed his story to paper. The trustworthiness of the details of his memory may therefore be open to question, although the strength of emotion suggests some degree of reliability.

   Little enough had been known heretofore about John Gulliver, except that he became governor of a workhouse and a minor government advisor, and in later life, was ordained a minister of the Church of England. He never married, but the scholar Faulkner Motte suggests that he may have had long relationships with two women, one considerably younger than himself. It seems that he disapproved of his sister Betty's marriage, which he considered beneath her, and he bequeathed the bulk of his tidy fortune towards building a bedlam institute. He also left sufficient funds to his housekeeper's children to enable them to complete their education. A scholarly appraisal of the edited and transcribed account reproduced here may be found in Faulkner Motte, 'An assessment of the provenance and reliability of John Gulliver's Notes from a Journal', The International Journal of Gulliver Studies, vol. 17 (26), October (2005), pp 45-60.

John Gulliver writes as follows:

I was always a 'good' child and my father proudly used to call me his 'towardly', or promising, Johnny. That was, of course, before the gloom set in and he turned against us all. He was pleased enough when I did well at grammar school. And when my sister Betty and I were little, he used to take great pride in Betty's needlework. She was never one for the books, but she was – still is - kindly and good-natured, and a great consolation to her mother. Those better equipped to judge appliqué embroidery than I were known to comment on her extraordinarily imaginative and exotic patterns and her attention to detail...

In those early days, our little family took Father's travels in good part - or at least I thought I did. Yet, embedded deep in my memory are scenes that now stir some doubt in me. I am reminded of a few occasions when mother thought we had retired to bed, and I came upon her staring through the drawing-room window, convulsed in tears. 'You're a good boy, John,' she had wept on one such occasion, stroking my arm, 'You deserve a father like every other boy.'

I knew full well that not every boy had a father any more than I: Billy Palmerston's was an army captain away in service, and Charles Ford's had died of diphtheria when we were eleven; the family fortune - and poor Charlie's prospects – were much narrowed as a result. I suppose I was thankful to Father that we were never left short. (Once I mentioned this in passing to Mother and she sniffed in disagreement. 'Humph!' she said, 'If he hadn't had my dowry it might have been an entirely different story!') Later I realised that Father's fortunes had flourished and that there was no economic necessity whatever for him to take off on his preposterous travels. That discovery, added to the niggardly feeling that Father was leaving to escape from us, not to support us, did little to instil self-worth in me.

I now realise how scanty are the memories I have of my father, and that in itself tells something. Those impressions that I have are coloured with more vivid and turbulent feeling than ought be expressed in polite society. But I beg you to

52

look at the issue from my point of view: look at the provocation I endured.
By the time I was nine or ten – long before his voyages brought him fame -
I had grown weary of hearing what an accomplished musician Lemuel Gulliver
had been as a child. How melodiously he played the spinet; what a mechanical
genius he had always possessed; how he had been so fine and scholarly a fellow
that he was sent to Emmanuel College in Cambridge when he was a mere
fourteen. Secretly, I shuddered with anxiety when I remembered that the fates
failed to reward him for his good behaviour or his devotion to his studies.
'Did I wallow in self-pity?' he used to ask rhetorically and with cold self-pity,
when he'd remind us how he was plucked from the haven of Cambridge and
ignominiously apprenticed to a surgeon. He would bitterly rage on the destiny
of third sons such as himself, who came from families with sins and sons more
numerous than fortunes. On my more expansive days, I imagined how miserable
that must have been for a youth so governed by reason as he was. Later, when
I had occasion and leisure to ponder these things, I wondered whether the
exposure at so tender an age to disease, to lumps of deformity, to the stench of
human innards and to the decay of dying left an indelible mark on the studious,
rather prim youth. (I fancy Father was a prim youth, inclined to know too much
for others to enjoy his company, and out of sympathy with humans even then.)
Mostly, however, I used to stiffen with resentment and silently accuse him of
visiting on Betty and myself the misery he himself suffered as a youth.

As time passed, I became a gangly youth and my blood boiled more easily
and rapidly. Those's how it is with young fellows, of course; but, believe me,
I suffered unique provocation. Can you imagine the humiliation I suffered on
realising that I was pitied by schoolmasters who 'made allowances' for certain
boys with absent fathers, and who included me in the category? Father once
accused me of being smitten with pride, and maybe I am. How often I clenched
my lips to stop myself lashing out against being pitied. Little did I realise that
worse ignominy than that was to come.

Worse than the shadowy absence, the blank space that I rushed to fill with benign and ill-conceived ideas about ideal fatherhood, was the rupture created by the wanderer's return. A whirlpool of hope - and terror - that Father would stay home this time, and anxiety that he might abandon us again, would consume me. If I were honest, I might admit that I probably always resented this intruder's – this stranger's - forays into Mother's predictable, orderly household. I resented his claim on her attentions in the early days when he touched her arm and whispered to her and when she blushed and treasured the trinkets he brought from early voyages.

Yet, however bad it was to be obliged to share Mother with him, what seared me to the quick was the effort of holding my head up in public. His travels took him to outlandish shores and inevitably his accounts of them became increasingly grotesque and bizarre. Long before he took to spending his days in the stables or permeating the house with the stench of horse, and leaving a trail of oats through the morning room, I was certain my friends were passing remarks about his eccentric, not so say wildish, traveller's tales. I had not failed to notice the way they gleefully and mercilessly poked fun at Jonathan Sutcliff's pater. He was a man from Nether Redriff known to favour malt whisky more than was good for him, and a neighbour had confided to the local grocer that Sutcliff senior had spent a night in a drunken stupor on the doorstep of the family home. Every time I saw boys cluster and whisper and guffaw, I imagined they were discussing Father's tales. The tall tale he told about boys and girls playing hide and seek in his hair in the place he called Lilliput particularly fuelled sullenness in me. Not only because it was preposterous and clearly an untruth (although of course that clearly was the case), but because - and I would not have admitted this back then – I wished that he would have played hide and seek with Betty and myself. Just once.

Did I fancy that the boys refused to meet my gaze after news spread of the Lilliput chronicles? Did their eyes bore into my back during lessons, or was that my wild imagining? When St John Manley suddenly ceased our regular Latin grammar study sessions in my home (St John and I had planned to go up to Oxford together and spent many evenings contriving word games and translating Cicero), I concluded that he was ashamed to be my friend. Years later I discovered that his father decided that it was more fitting for a shopkeeper's son to learn to cipher and to count than to do declensions, but how was I to know that then? Father's talk had first met with wonder and amazement, and because of his reputation as a decent, truthful man, it was given some credence. And it was rumoured that the headmaster of Rotherhithe Grammar School – my own school - had called to hear an account of the enlightened educational system of the Lilliputians while I was taking the air at my Uncle John's home after a bad bout of the croup.

Father had displayed considerable interest in certain aspects of education, and was anxious to share them with anyone who would listen. Lilliputian parents, he informed us, are the last of all to be trusted with the education of their own children. They are discouraged from fondling or indulging their young and are encouraged to place them in communal nurseries and school, to be returned home only at a marriageable age, or when they are to be apprenticed or prepared for trade, as befits their status. However, in Lilliput removing the children from their homes does not remove from parents the financial burden children generate. As Father pithily put it to the good Dr Marsh, our headmaster, 'nothing can be more unjust, than for people, in subservience to their own appetites, to bring children into the world, and leave the burthen of supporting them on the public'. Father deduced from this philosophy that children should not be under any obligation to their fathers for begetting them, or to their mothers for bringing them into the world.

My father would probably be pleased to know that I applaud the rationality of the Lilliputians. I am struck by the boldness of their determination to instill bravery and sound sense into their young women, rather than foolishness and

SEEK

The tall tale he told about boys and girls playing **hide** and **seek** in his hair in the place he called Lilliput particularly fuelled sullenness in me. Not only because it was preposterous and clearly an untruth (although of course that clearly was the case), but because - and I would not have admitted this back then – I wished that he would have played hide and seek with Betty and myself. Just once.

frivolity. However, more than this, I could not then help but think how Father himself had followed the spirits of the Lilliputian educational tenets. After all, he had entrusted his children into the care of whomsœver, and indeed he did dispense the debts that begetting children incurred. True, Mother had thwarted the purity of his plan. She insisted on irrational affection and selfless dedication to her young. But Father was true to his principle of not spoiling or indulging us. And, after his trip to Houyhnhnmland, that country inhabited by the rational and noble race of horses and the brutish Yahoos whom he believed were endowed with the worst vices of human beings, of even noticing our existence at all.

I am told that our esteemed headmaster left our home bewildered after hearing his treatise on the Lilliputian education system. He was spared my intimate knowledge of Father's daily congress with horses and the so-called rational disquisitions that provoked.

Long before Father found more solace in horses than in his own family, our acquaintances in Redriff took a sceptical view of his deepening eccentricities. The summer he had returned from Brobdingnag, there was no mistaking the boys' whispered allusions to his strangeness. That was the year I realised he had gone too far. He was not ten days at home when he contrived excuses to leave again. Mother protested he should never go to sea any more. I read in his book that he obtained her consent because he claimed it would enhance his children's prospects. Well, yes. That was so. But not exactly as he supposed.

Let me explain. We had just taken a rather comely scullery maid into service (she had a way of throwing a cheeky sideways glance that was simultaneously distinctly discomfiting and beguiling), but her downfall was her loose tongue. The day of Father's return from his voyage into the unknown, it was our misfortune that she opened the door to him, and she skulked in the hallway during the whole sorry homecoming. I know for a fact that she was the one responsible for spreading word in the neighbourhood about his shameful behaviour. I still burn with mortification when I think of it. First he affected to have forgotten where our house was or the configuration of the region, and had the gall to ask his way home of several neighbours. The Hobbs's governess, the drapier on Green Street, and Martin Ludder, a local clergyman, told us so themselves. As if that was not bad enough, he repeatedly and haughtily admonished them – his former friends and neighbours - to clear the way for him. I need hardly tell you that this did not go down well. Next, he got it into his head that we had all shrunk in size, although I had grown a full four inches in his absence and Betty was turning into a grand young woman. I was outraged when he accused poor mother of ſtarving us – mother, who prided herself on her fine table, with loins of mutton and joints of beef on the sideboard at every repaſt and gallons of cream sent regularly from the dairy! It didn't take long to figure out that he had loſt his wits. Temporarily, Mother said. But the truth is that he was never the same again.

The fact of the matter is that his rapid departure on yet another dubious odyssey was a blessed relief to us all. After he had spent a week on dry land, a week filled for me with fending off enquiries about his ſtate of mind and suffering Sutcliff's sneers, I prevailed on Mother to consent to his departure, and an unhappy peace descended on us. Thereafter she seemed to harden. Certainly, there were no more teary intervals.

Father did return again to the fold, with fanciful tales of Laputa and Balnibarbi and Japan, and he ſtayed home for a full five months. I conceded to an uneasy truce; by then I was more intereſted in what victuals were offered on the dinner table and how I could conspire to spend time alone in my chambers, in the way of sullen youths. The household had juſt learned to accommodate his edgy presence when, inevitably, another offer of a voyage materialised, and before you could say Robinson Crusœ, the maid was filling his trunk with linens. Six months after his departure mother gave birth to a sickly, squalling infant girl. I couldn't but note how little thought the child's begetter accorded the shred of life he had created. And when, on a Tuesday morning six weeks after her arrival

John Hassall

into this world – the previous day the babe had responded to my customary scowl with a wisp of a smile - mother found her, unaccountably, cold and blue in her cradle. A cold rush of fury overtook me. Years later, when I read Father's book and noted how he failed to mention a word about her beyond her imminent arrival as he departed, that chill tore my soul once more. I noted too his comment that 'one half of our natives were good for nothing but bringing children into the world; and to trust the care of our children to such useless animals,' he had continued, 'was yet a greater instance of brutality.' Indeed.

I don't need to remind you of the details of his voyages. You are probably more familiar with them than I. Within days of his book being published in 1726, his tale was on the lips of high and low, from the housekeeper's son's to the little royal princesses'. But there are some details from Father's ramblings that held a particular resonance for me, snippets that stayed fast in the memory of an impressionable, resentful, boy who was effectively fatherless. For instance, while I laid plans for my own future at the dining table in Redriff, I couldn't help but note that apparently inconsequential lads played an important part in the fantastic adventures of Father's reports. Nameless young fellows with no voices – the kind one might scarcely notice on the streets of Redriff – actually steered the action and the actors of the famous voyages in one direction or another or were favoured by Providence. There was the nameless cabin-boy whom fate had arbitrarily and momentarily favoured. In 1710, as I recall, on the high seas my father had encountered a ship from Bristol captained by a man named Pocock. Father later learned that a storm cost the lives of all Pocock's crew – except this solitary cabin-boy. Did the boy deserve his fate any more or less than his fellows who were lost? Or than I, the neglected offspring of a scowling, public man? Remember the Brobdingnagian pageboy who ambled off to filch birds' eggs instead of caring for Father? Had he not done so, Lemuel Gulliver might never have relinquished the infantile comforts of the giant-land of Brobdingnag, and I might never again have laid eyes on him. It took his light-hearted negligence of duty to return Father to his adult senses, or what he had left of them. It was while the pageboy pursued his mischievous plans, that Father, left unattended, was plucked by an eagle from his infantile security in Brobdingnag, dropped into the ocean and rescued by an English ship. And thus he found his passage home for a brief respite.

Then there were the boys who climbed the masts and sighted land (one such is the boy who discovered Brobdingnag). What power those lads held! As much as – perhaps even more than – the captains of their ships! It was they who decided on the course of the venture; their cries of 'Land ahoy!' or their carelessly overlooking distant shores made all the difference. It seemed to me that although Father mentioned them in passing, it was as if he was hardly ever aware of their existence. From his perspective, they were incidentals, as important as any other piece of machinery on the ship, but of as little consequence. Yet, to them we owe the bones of the Gulliver story. I recall, too, how Father sometimes mused about what wars might have been averted had not a little royal Lilliputian unidentified to history cut his finger when topping his egg. Father's reflections on this matter led me to parallel speculations: would the wars of the Big-endians and the Little-endians have seemed less ludicrous to him had they been predicated on a gash to an adult, rather than a childish, finger? It seemed as if children's agency was ridiculed. What all this taught me was that we are all the stars' tennis balls, but that chance alone seems to govern especially the destinies of children.

See how it altered the life of a nine-year old simple farmer's daughter from Brobdingnag. The effect of meeting my father was that Glumdalclitch, a mere child, acquired wisdom and responsibility beyond her years. In her dealings with my father, adult-child roles were, ironically, reversed. My father was transformed into a plaything, a docile passive creature, anxious to please an inconsequential country child. She became a nurse, a servant, a confidant, a teacher of manners and languages, a protector of my father's dignity and modesty… Father, the great explorer, the great rationaliser, was literally and metaphorically tied to her

Louis Rhead

apron strings. Not only were adult cares thrust on her, but she was plucked from her rural blameless life and cast into the intrigues of the royal court. And every royal court resembles the flying island of Laputa that Father droned on about, in that its subjects are preoccupied with absurd projects and manners, and neglect useful, worthwhile pursuits. Here at the royal court, it seems, she learned to be 'arch', as Father puts it. Manipulative, I would say. How heavily should that moral twist weigh on Father's conscience, I wonder? Did the adult Glumdalclitch become a wily, ingratiating courtier, living on her wits? Did she succumb to the licentiousness and chicanery of court life that erodes all decency? Certainly, there was no going back for her, no return to a simple life. Was she therefore doomed to spend her days between two warring worlds, the old artless, humble one she had abandoned in my father's interests, and the scheming, arch bubble into which she was catapulted?

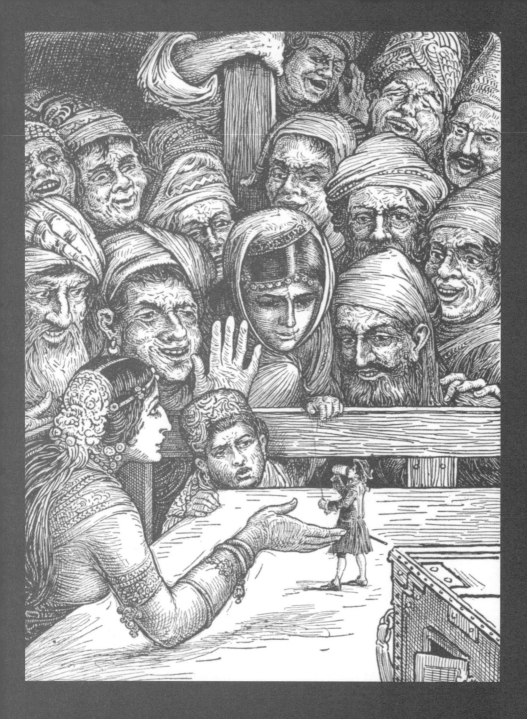

Louis Rhead

Thomas Morten

Anonymous illustrator [1890s]

It was a man I never met and I know little about, a man called Don Pedro of Lisbon, who was the final arbiter of the fate of my family. It was he who put it upon Father, as a matter of honour and conscience, as Father said, that he ought to 'return to his native country, and live at home with his wife and children.' A great one for truth, honour and conscience was Lemuel Gulliver; that much is clear from his book. A great one, too, for grand ſtatements: 'Principally,' he often used to proclaim, 'I hate and deteſt that animal called man; although I heartily love John, Peter, Thomas.' Many's the time he undertook to prove his case by force of argument. However, the experiences of this particular John, his own son, did little to prove the truth of his fine dictum.

I eventually managed to escape the moral high tone of Father's house in Redriff, where the horses in the ſtables were accorded more dignity than the women and children of the household. Emmanuel College Cambridge did not beckon me, sadly, nor Oxford. Inſtead, I was lucky to be accepted in a minor inſtitution on the godforsaken neighbouring island entitled Trinity College. There I was accorded a discreditable mark at the end of my ſtudies, and my 'dullness and insufficiency' were the subject of some debate. Little wonder that I should conclude that my childhood became the type of all my future disappointments.

This is a fictional account woven around details from Gulliver's Travels *and from the life of Jonathan Swift.*

J.J. Grandville

I V

Picturing GULLIVER

Valerie Coghlan

Did Jonathan Swift realise what a legacy he would leave when he wrote *Gulliver's Travels*? It has been translated into many languages, the terms 'Lilliput' and 'Lilliputian' have entered the vocabulary of people who have probably never even heard of Swift, and anyone referred to as a 'yahoo' knows it is not flattering. The bizarre adventures of the prosaic English surgeon, Lemuel Gulliver, have amused and entranced for nearly 300 years, stretching imagination and summoning mental pictures of places and people that are probably, in the most literal sense, outside the wildest dreams of most people. But it takes no imaginative leap to grasp that Swift's accounts of the places visited by Gulliver are fertile material for artists. The earliest editions were illustrated by a portrait of Lemuel Gulliver and maps, supposedly providing credence for his voyages. Then simple wood-block illustration began to appear, in the style of the late 1700s and early nineteenth century, but once the means of illustrating books became more sophisticated as the nineteenth century progressed, artists began with gusto to mine the possibilities presented by Swift.

This article discusses some of the better known, and a few lesser-known, illustrated volumes of *Gulliver's Travels*. It is by no means a survey, nor is it completely comprehensive. That would require a book to itself in that there are well over a hundred illustrated editions, ranging from the 'arty' collectors' items, a few of which are discussed below, to simplified versions, often crudely illustrated, some of which are firmly aimed at schools' markets. One thing is sure though: this story of a man cast into strange worlds, sometimes a giant and sometimes diminutive, sometimes a semi-civilised creature, a man coping with extraordinary circumstances, which in his fumbling way, he tries to rationalise, has an enduring power over its readers.

Illustrations of the story vary from interpretations by some of the great illustrators of the past 200 years – Rackham, Pogány, Bawden and many more - to hack work provided for cheap editions, often simple retellings specifically for children. According to Humphrey Carpenter, one of the first editions for children was published by Benjamin Tabert in London in 1805, with three coloured copperplates. The majority of illustrators of *Gulliver's Travels* represent rather than

René Bull

interpret the text in that they show what people and places looked like without enlarging too much on Swift's own quite visual text; in this they illuminate rather than expand his words in the manner of a true picturebook. Perhaps Swift's fertile imagination is sufficiently rich to need little embellishment. F.J. Harvey Darton, who edited the volume illustrated by René Bull, comments in his introduction that 'Gulliver's bubbles have not burst [referring to the South Sea Bubble which burst *circa* 20 years after Gulliver's voyages]. Though fictitious, they are too true to break, and even if they were not, they make so real a picture that they cannot be pricked'.

Most of the illustrators discussed make Gulliver look like a real individual rather than a caricature, even when, as in Horst Lemke's and Hans Baltzer's drawings he is a cartoon-like character. Many artists have been unable to resist romanticising him; mostly he is shown with dark hair, firm jaw, and in some case striking good looks, while J. J. Grandville, Alexander King and V.A. Poirson show an earthier, more bucolic surgeon, and unusually, Poirson's Gulliver is blond. A.E. Jackson's Gulliver looks quite effeminate at times; something

played up when, unusually among the illustrators of *Gulliver's Travels*, he shows Don Pedro taking leave of Gulliver. True to the text, Don Pedro is shown embracing Gulliver, leaning in towards him, while Gulliver who 'bore [this] as well I could' keeps his arms straight by his side and looks prim. The rather girlish good looks of R.G. Mossa's Gulliver is intensified in some scenes: we observe Gulliver dancing in Lilliput and carefully taking off his stockings before he enters the sea, and elsewhere gazing dreamily over Lilliput. Even when he is pulling the boats to Lilliput, he looks more like an eager boy than a qualified doctor and a husband.

Generally, illustrators have chosen to stick to a late seventeenth- or eighteenth-century setting of *Gulliver's Travels*, and he is shown dressed more or less appropriately for the period, unlike other classic stories, such as *Alice's Adventures in Wonderland*, where period setting varies in illustrated versions. Perhaps the supposedly factual narration of Gulliver's journeys imposes a desire to further the notion of authenticity on the part of illustrators, and the places visited by Gulliver do allow for imaginative visual play, even while remaining faithful to the text. It is remarkable too that many artists have chosen to depict the same scenes, and this will be discussed in more detail further on in this essay. Undoubtedly, these are the great set-pieces of the book, and in particular in the earlier voyages, and it is interesting to speculate to what extent our inner picture of Gulliver, for example pinned to the ground by his hair as well as with ropes, has been reinforced by the constant redepiction of a broadly similar image.

While many of the illustrated versions of *Gulliver's Travels* have been prepared for a juvenile audience, there are quite a few that are unlikely to appeal to a particularly young audience, and there are a few that are very adult indeed, such as James Millar's highly stylised Grecian figures. Seemingly etched in white on a black background, a touch of Beardsley here intensifying a self-conscious note of decadence about the mostly nude figures, we see Gulliver reclining languorously in Lilliput, and the Houyhnhnms with their humanised heads are satyrs. Some of these editions are produced for a limited edition or fine art market, like the Cresset Press edition (1930) illustrated by Rex Whistler in pen and ink and reproduced

by photogravure, very consciously intending to give an 'authentic' feel for the period. An ornate map announces 'The Kingdoms of Lilliput and Blefuscu discovered by Mr Lemuel Gulliver in 1699', a number of single-page pictures of Gulliver are framed memento-style by an intricate interworking of objects relevant to the scene as well as a skull, always giving a sense of historical distance to the story, and when we look closely, we realise that sometimes Whistler is nudging us towards how we might regard Gulliver in a particular situation: we note a mermaid and merman looking wryly at each other as they frame sailors heading towards Gulliver in his box on the waves, and a similar pair of mer people along with other classical figures provide unspoken comments on others of his exploits.

The two-volume Golden Cockerel edition illustrated by David Jones's woodcuts, is equally consciously arty with its seemingly simple maps, gently coloured and beautifully lettered, and enlivened by ships, mermaids and other figures. The influence of Eric Gill, with whom Jones was closely associated, is evident in these beautifully made volumes. The 1929 Limited Editions Club volume illustrated

Thomas Morten

Willy Pogány

J.G. Thomson

by Alexander King's images in shades of black, grey brown and sepia look as if they belong in a graphic novel. The coarser aspects of the story are emphasised: Gulliver is shown squatting behind a wall to relieve himself while his waste is carried off in wheelbarrows by bewigged servants, the child about to devour Gulliver is terrifying and his Yahoos are horrific. All of these editions, and others, point up the adult potential that this story still holds, and cause regret that now it is a tale often relegated to the junior shelves of book shops and libraries.

J.J. Grandville's 1838 edition presents an imaginative capturing of the intentions of Swift that still has the power to amaze and even shock. Born Jean Ignace-Isadore Gérard in Nancy in 1803; at the age of 20 he went to Paris where he quickly established a reputation as a political cartoonist and lithographer; he is also noted for his fine lines and the quality of the wood engravings made by highly skilled craftsmen from his drawings. Stringent censorship laws, however, turned him away from political satire and towards the less risky work of an illustrator of classic texts. In 1838 his illustrated version of *Fables de La Fontaine* was published and

quickly followed in the same year by *Voyages de Gulliver dans les Contrées Lointaines*. In some scenes Grandville gives relatively literal interpretations of Swift's narrative, especially in the earlier voyages, but elsewhere his fascination with the bizarre and phantasmagoric reign supreme. This is most evident in his depiction of the Yahoos, described by Denis Donoghue in his foreword to a 1988 reissue of the Grandville volume, as 'appalling'. The 'Rudiments of Lewdness, Coquetry, Censure and Scandal' displayed by female Yahoos are given full reign; most notably lewdness is to the fore when a Yahoo female displays her desire for Gulliver. Donoghue comments that 'he [Grandville] is more disconcertingly revealed in drawings which show nature not confounded so much as imperturbably grotesque', and quotes Baudelaire 'when I step into the work of Grandville some sort of disquiet takes hold of me'. Grandville's skill as an artist is showcased too in the many vignettes and visual asides that embellish his pages, but it is undoubtedly in his grasp of Swift's black humour that he excels; William Makepeace Thackeray, also an illustrator, called Grandville 'the Swift of the pencil', and it could be speculated that an affinity of mind between author and illustrator may be explained when we learn that Grandville died insane in 1847.

In the 1865 edition, illustrated by T. Morten, the political overtones in the story are referenced in 'explanatory notes and a life of the author by John Francis Waller, LL.D.'. Morten, whose illustrations for most of the leading journals of his time were well-known, was a good match for this edition of Swift's work; he emphasises the political satire at play in some of the scenes, particularly in the life of Dean Swift, also illustrated, which prefaces the travels, and in Gulliver's discourse with his Houyhnhnm master; they are credited by Houfe as Morten's finest illustrations. Morten's incisive drawings and Christ Riddell's cartoonish interpretation published over 100 years later are probably the most overtly political images to accompany Swift's words, both artists showing their paces as leading political satirists.

Morten's crowd scenes are very detailed, and some sly touches are only appreciated on very close looking. His Lilliputian world has a European flavour, medieval at times with its crooked buildings and heavily armoured knights, and the court of Lilliput suggests seventeenth-century Spain, elaborate and courtly, providing Morten with ample opportunity to show fine details. When Gulliver recounts that the Lilliputians 'made an exact inventory of everything they saw', we see that as well as recording everything in writing (just as Morten shows this scene in great visual detail), they also painted a portrait of their enormous visitor, and in the bottom left of the illustration a little figure appears under the hood of a camera pointing at Gulliver. Unlike Grandville, Morten has preferred to concentrate on illustrating the Houyhnhnms, giving much less emphasis to the Yahoos, perhaps not surprising in an edition that has been bowdlerised.

Other distinguished artists of the later nineteenth century who illustrated *Gulliver's Travels* included Gordon Browne, son of Hablôt K. Browne, 'Phiz', best-known for his illustrations of Dickens's books. Browne, a prolific illustrator and regarded by critics as a better artist than his father, worked on many classic stories, *The Boys' Own Paper* and *The Girls' Own Paper*, boys' adventure stories and some

J.J. Grandville

of the novels of Irish writer, L.T. Meade. The influence of *Japonisme* and oriental art may be seen to excellent effect in the illustrations of French artist V.A. Poirson. The costumes of his Lilliputians and their buildings and artefacts are Japanese in style; his palette is predominately yellow and orange; watercolour is applied lightly to his delicately drawn figures, some of whom almost dance across the pages, emphasising the energy and intensity of movement he imparts to the characters and their air of busyness as little figures occupy themselves attending to Gulliver, as in a scene where they prepare his food. Like many other artists, he has lavished most effort on the scenes where dozens of minute people almost buzz around the giant in their midst. Looking at a variety of editions of *Gulliver's Travels* the impression comes across that overall, artists have most enjoyed illustrating a giant in a small world rather than episodes from later in the book. If you can call a giant discreet, Poirson's Gulliver is a little more discreetly shown than in some other editions. Just his head is visible as he pulls the Blefuscu boats to shore, and his face is concealed by his large-brimmed hat in some earlier scenes. Poirson also shows

some of the less-dramatic moments, like the Lilliputians pulling Gulliver's hat along as he is carried on a platform on wheels. Poirson's Brobdingnagians are Abyssinian warriors, with moustaches and turbans, and a magnificently bearded king, and his sense of costume has imaginative reign when it comes to the magically-cloaked Laputians. Nevertheless, his ability to draw what a garment conceals is evident where we view brawling naked Yahoos, and the delicacy of his line does not mask the physical power of his kindly-disposed Houyhnhnms. Poirson uses the somewhat elongated pages of this edition to advantage too; some illustrations are full page, but others sprawl diagonally between blocks of print with an artless air, while emphasising whatever action is pictured.

Like Poirson, and other artists of the *fin-de siècle*, Arthur Rackham was attracted to Japanese art, and while his costumes and artefacts are less definitively oriental than Poirson's, throughout the travels Japanese fans, dress and other artefacts and touches of eastern style are evident. Rackham's first approach to Gulliver was in a volume of black and white drawings published in 1899, and subsequently another edition containing

12 colour plates was issued in 1937. The illustrations are dated 1909. The publishers supply a note to the 1937 edition stating that 'the designs … were subsequently worked over, revised and coloured by the artist, and some new designs added'. Rackham's characteristic style is to the fore in the scenes in Brobdingnag; the small man in a giant world gives him most scope for the air of concealed threat that permeates much of his best work. We see Gulliver 'struck with fear' at the sight of the Brobdingnagian reapers; the palette is typically dark, browns and blacks, heightening the air of menace, and as in so many of Rackham's illustrations, suggesting much more than is obvious at first glance; his battle with giant wasps is dramatic and fearsome too; in these scenes he is shown in 'normal' size, vulnerable in a giant world, while his struggle with the frog is shown from the perspective of the Brobdingnagian ladies, emphasising his smallness. Rackham's ability to toggle between looming threat and lightness is shown when the frog, no longer menacing, acts as an aside in playful vignettes.

The first quarter of the twentieth century saw a number of the foremost illustrators of the time responding to the lure of illustrating *Gulliver's Travels*. Louis John Rhead was one of these. Rhead was born in England, trained as an artist in South Kensington and Paris, but did most of his illustrative work in America where he established himself as a graphic designer and illustrator of posters as well as books. Rhead provided 100 black and white drawings for this edition, but it is his frontispiece of Gulliver emerging like a colossus from the sea that has become one of the enduring images of the tale. He is known as a realistic illustrator, but in *Gulliver's Travels* he allows himself some flights of fancy – or fantasy. His drawings are finely detailed, some more amusing and reflecting the spirit of the narrative than others, such as the scene where he shows the sliced-open heads of Balnabarbi politicians.

Some of these artists were not specialists in illustrating books for a young audience, but a more discernible focus on child readers is noticeable at this period. American illustrator Milo Winter is clearly conscious that in his depictions of the travels he is aiming at children; the sense of menace evident in earlier editions, even in those intended for younger readers, is absent. This, also, of course, reflects a

Arthur Rackham

BATTLE OF THE RATS

society, at least in America and Britain where most of the editions discussed were published, that is moving towards publications with very specific child appeal. John Hassall's illustrations appear in an edition 'retold for little folk by Agnes Grozier Herbertson'. Hassall, born in England, studied art in Antwerp and Paris. On his return to Britain, he established his reputation as a designer of posters and greeting cards, a form and style he adapted well to illustrating children's books. His skill in appealing to children was also honed by illustrating comics and boys' adventure stories. His line is clear and bold, and his colours flat, giving a somewhat two-dimensional effect to his illustration, especially his colour work. In *Gulliver's Travels* some of his best work is in the black and white drawings, which simply yet effectively catch mood, as in the scene where the Lilliputians scheme against Gulliver who stands back-turned, distanced, and therefore equal in stature to his accusers, or where again viewed from the back, the Brobdingnagian servant lies distraught as an eagle makes off with the box containing Gulliver. In contrast, some of the colour illustrations are stereotypical, lacking emotional as well as physical depth, unlike the black and white drawings where there is a greater sense of an artist catching the feelings of his subjects. In colour, comic moments are better depicted by Hassall, for example a hint of burlesque in the scene where the Brobdingnagian farmer and his wife examine Gulliver. This also illustrates the cover of the retelling illustrated by Hassall, and commonly from here on some form of coloured cover, engraved, laid on picture-plate or dust jacket, sets out to attract readers to many of the editions of *Gulliver's Travels*.

It is not a surprise that Hungarian artist, Vilmos Andreas, 'Willy' Pogány illustrated an edition of *Gulliver's Travels*; it is edited by Padraic Colum, the illustrations for whose books are among Pogány's best known work. Pogány, one of the most popular illustrators of his time in the United States, was also well-regarded for his decorative work and film set and stage design. His early influences included Hungarian peasant art and Chinese and Japanese decorative art. Later, he developed an interest in Art Nouveau. These influences may be seen in his Gulliver, particularly vibrantly in scenes in Laputa and Lagado, where the deliberations of mathematicians and painters mixing colours by feeling and smelling offered Pogány glowing opportunities to show his talents as a designer and colourist, in particular the geometric designs surrounding the mathematicians resonate with all of the impact of a stage set. In contrast, some of his pen and ink sketches are plain and restrained at first glance, but they are equally telling, for example, in showing the antagonism of the small- and big-endians, their conviction of their own rightness emphasised by the neck stocks worn by each, indicating the authority of church and state. The sad and depressed Struldbruggs are sympathetically captured in a few pen-strokes; these are not the grotesque creatures of Alexander King or more recently Riddell, rather they are more akin to Rackham's aged creature, reflecting their despair at the prospect of so much longevity.

The impact of art and fashions from different parts of the world, and especially from what might broadly be termed 'the east', i.e. east of America and Western Europe, is noticeable in book illustration at the end of the nineteenth and early twentieth century. Lemuel Gulliver's travels to unknown lands and exotic eastern parts gave artists plenty of scope to display their knowledge and interest. René Bull, who was born in Dublin in 1872, was influenced by oriental art, and was an expert in Arab customs and costumes, which he demonstrates to full-advantage in his admired *Arabian Nights* (1912) and *Rubáiyát of Omar Kyhhám* (1913). His Lilliputians and Brobdingnagians have a Cossack air about them, and buildings have onion domes and minarets. He is one of a few artists who show a bearded Gulliver. F. J. Harvey Darton who edited this edition notes that *Gulliver's Travels* may be seen 'as a picture of the real sea-life of the day', and Bull's depiction of the travels is definitely realistic, unlike some of other twentieth-century artists who began to show a more stylised and fanciful backdrop and even depictions of Gulliver himself, possibly with a view to emphasising the appeal of the fantastic in a story for children. At this stage, *Gulliver's Travels* was regarded largely as a children's book, but what age children, and indeed what sort of children, were expected to read it shows in variations in the illustrations in different editions and their likely appeal to a young audience.

V. A. Poirson

J.J. Grandville

An edition illustrated by Edwin John Prittie was published in the USA at much the same time as the edition illustrated by Bull, but this is for a younger readership, with more amusing elements of the story played up, in particular in the colour illustrations, and like some other artists who used a mixture of colour and black and white, it is the seemingly plainer drawings that are more dramatically vigorous.

Edward Bawden was one of the most highly-regarded English illustrators and designers of his age; his techniques included line drawing, woodcuts and lithography and he was also noted as a watercolourist and a designer of ceramic tiles, murals and posters. His eye for an arresting angle in a picture would have served him well in his murals and poster designs, and in his *Gulliver's Travels* his play on perspective brings a new interpretation to scenes that may be over-familiar. He shows Gulliver from the Lilliputian point of view, with mighty legs and trunk and a smaller head as his body recedes into the distance. Especially striking are the stylised images of Gulliver stepping over the city walls and sitting at his table, winching up tiny barrels of wine.

Bawden illustrated the first two journeys of the travels, and the voyages to Lilliput and Brobdingnag, or the voyage to Lilliput alone, tend to feature solely in post-1940 editions. Also dealing with the first two journeys, Robin Jacques's edition in black and white ink, touched with very delicate washes of blue and brown in places, are arresting, showing close-up juxtaposing of large heads and small bodies, or even legs and feet which is all we see of a Brobdingnagian to whom Gulliver attempts to explain himself. Nevertheless, these stippled and cross-hatched images are, like those of Edward Bawden, more likely to have adult or young adult rather than child appeal. But waves that pound Gulliver's ship as it lurches to the rocks will ring true with any viewer, and the tightly focused image of Gulliver's head as he regards his tiny captors also offers insights into the predicament of Lemuel Gulliver. These, and subsequent editions of *Gulliver's Travels*, benefited from post-World War Two developments in photolithographic processes, giving Jacques in his 'Gulliver' the latitude to create in fine pen, drawings that resemble wood engravings.

Further developments in lithographic printing are evident in the quality of colour and print in two outstanding editions of *Gulliver's Travels* published in the 1960s and illustrated by two German picturebook artists. Erich Kästner, author of the 'Emil' books, retells the first two voyages in the edition of *Gullivers Reisen* illustrated by Horst Lemke. Lemke, born in Berlin in 1922 and a runner up for the Hans Christian Andersen Medal, also illustrated a number of other books by Kästner. Lemke's fluid line is spiky and stylised, serving to heighten the humour of the story, especially in the colour scenes. Other scenes are shown as black and white sketches, full of lively detail too, giving emphasis to the dramatic as well as the less serious side of the story. The edition illustrated by Hans Baltzer, also born in Berlin, in 1900, was originally published in German, but subsequently Baltzer's images were teamed with an English edition edited by Elaine Moss. Like the Lemke edition, this is a large format publication, no doubt suiting Baltzer, who, we are told in a cover note about the illustrator, has trouble fitting his drawings on to a page. Undoubtedly, Baltzer uses his pages to full effect,

sometimes surrounding the text with his visual interpretations. His line is strong and vigorous, in contrast to his colours, which though bright are delicately applied, giving force to scenes like that of the Brobdingnagian frog encroaching on Gulliver whose viewpoint the observer shares, as he cowers back from the hideous monster. His double-page spreads are especially arresting, whether it is Gulliver roped and helpless in Lilliput, pulling the Blefuscuian ships to shore, or observed on a table top by amused Brobdingnagians, but in particular the scene where his box is rescued from the waves, evokes empathy with Gulliver adrift on a wide sea.

The appeal of Gulliver for children was well-established by the 1960s, and not just within English-language publishing as we have seen with the two German editions discussed above. Swift's narrative has had wide appeal in France also; it has been illustrated by several French artists, and editions for children containing some of Grandville's artwork have also been published in the past 50 years. Looking at illustrated versions of *Gulliver's Travels* it is worth noting that while it was written in English, many of the artists

Thomas Morten

who have illustrated it have not been from Anglophone backgrounds. Victor Ambrus who illustrated Michæl West's 1963 retelling, and subsequently James Riordan's 1992 retellings of the first two voyages is, like Willy Pogány, Hungarian. Born in Budapest in 1935, he came to England in 1956 after the Hungarian uprising in that year. Ambrus was one of a number of illustrators taken up by the Oxford University Press in the 1960s, specifically to produce high-quality picturebooks, taking advantage of a revolution in colour reproduction. Ambrus's style is energetic and dramatic. Drawing horses is a strength of his, and early in his career he feared that he would become known only as an expert illustrator of equine subjects. It is, however, a pity given his expertise in this area, that he didn't get a chance to illustrate the Houyhnhnms. His line is in places bold and vigorous, but elsewhere delicate and intricate, as in the scenes in Lilliput where ornate details on buildings and in Lilliputian costume is finely limned. Commenting on Ambrus's work, Douglas Martin says 'Victor Ambrus is a brilliant colourist, though not in a painterly sense, since whenever one looks closely into the colour, irrespective of how it has been

applied, it will be found to be informed and underpinned by sound draughtsmanship in line'.

Gennady Spirin was born in Moscow in 1948, but moved to the United States to further his work as an artist. Stylistically he is quite unlike Ambrus, but is similar in his minute attention to detail. His work is self-consciously painterly, each page opening suggesting that here is a picture meant for hanging on a wall. This is a retelling of the Lilliput episode only by Ann Keay Benneduce, and the text is relatively short. Spirin's palette is muted: shades of terracotta and brown dominating many scenes, sometimes intensified by a blue background of sea or sky. While his illustrations look formal at a glance, anything more than that will show that he invests his characters with humour and there is a great sense of activity and movement in all scenes.

An edition published in 2002 in the United States is worth noting only because of its illustrations – the text is reduced to the point of banality. Germano Ovani does, however, with his light line and delicate colour capture visually something of Gulliver's exploits in Lilliput and Brobdingnag. The most recent edition

V. A. Poirson

of any visual significance of *Gulliver's Travels* to be published in English is illustrated by political satirist Chris Riddell and is discussed in detail elsewhere in this volume.

One of the most striking things arising from looking at a number of illustrated *Gulliver's Travels* is that artists have, in general, chosen the same scenes to illustrate. Of course these are key moments in the text, and the dramatic possibilities of some of them are very alluring to an artist. While some but not all, show Gulliver emerging from the shipwreck that casts him on Lilliput, none has missed Gulliver tied down, hair in hanks, pinioned to the ground, and earnestly examined by Lilliputians. Gulliver drawing the Blefuscu ships to the shores of Lilliput is also visually present in the editions discussed here, despite the time artists must have invested in the finer details of the ships' rigging. Also, he is shown by most of the illustrators discussed in some variant of the scene where he holds the Lilliputian king in his hand or where Lilliputians in their carriages parade around his dining table. Generally the Brobdingnagian farmers exclaiming in surprise at their minute visitor are visually captured, and other popular scenes from the Brobdingnagian episode include Gulliver falling into a bowl of cream or battling with a frog, and again many illustrators show the eagle carrying off Gulliver in his box home. Of course, these scenes offer illustrators an opportunity for dramatic play with concepts of large and small, and the Lilliputian illustrations in particular have provided a number of artists considerable opportunities in their depictions of the 'crowd scenes' in Lilliput. There is something quite cinematic about these scenes, and, for example, Gulliver roped to the ground or scrutinised by giant farmers act as establishing shots that set the scene for what comes next.

Gulliver is shown urinating on the fire in the Lilliputian queen's apartments in several editions. Poirson views him from the back, delicately holding out his jacket with one hand; Riddell also offers a back view, but this time Gulliver casts a furtive glance at the reader over one shoulder. Grandville protects Gulliver's modesty with a pillar, while in Alexander King's robust version, Gulliver unleashes a gush that would surely have flooded Lilliput. This episode is excised from some editions, in particular the more recent retellings for younger readers. The Martin Jenkins and Chris Riddell edition retains it however, as does a 1990s edition illustrated by Martin Hargreaves.

Artists have found splendid opportunity to play with colour and design throughout *Gulliver's Travels*, and it is obvious that some illustrators have enjoyed picturing the inventive artefacts encountered by Gulliver, especially in the later voyages. This is especially evident in the nineteenth-century editions, reflecting a contemporary preoccupation with science and invention. One incident captured with variations in a number of editions concerns the transfer of parts of politicians' brains in the Lagado Academy, so that reasonable agreement could be reached by means of political arguments taking place within their skulls. Various means by which this might have taken place are suggested visually: from Grandville who favours a vertical cranial incision to Rhead and Morten who show a horizontal incision, enabling the crown to be removed, thus facilitating the exchange of brain matter.

Inevitably, scrutiny of so many editions of *Gulliver's Travels* raises the question of whether Swift has found his ideal pictorial companion. Most, if not all, of the editions discussed here are remarkably faithful to the text, directing the reader's gaze to elaborations of the incidents depicted, but in general, not adding very much. Possibly the richness of Swift's own imagination in its descriptions of Gulliver's voyages has been a restraint. There is a sense that Arthur Rackham has not approached his subject matter here with his normal gusto, and an obligation to the text can be detected in the work of other artists. An edition published in 1864 with wood-engravings designed by J.G. Thomson adds a comic dimension to some events, especially those involving the Houyhnhnms, and Riddell and King also see a humorous side to the horse-like creatures who are more frequently portrayed as noble. J.J. Grandville has extended somewhat the grotesque elements of the story, and scenes are invested with his own obsessions with nightmarish fantasies. Denis Donoghue comments that Grandville has brought his own fascination with eyes, which he called 'les tours de force de l'esprit', to Swift's text, his close-up depiction of an eye directing its gaze to its subject, inviting the reader to gaze also on that subject.

Abridged and edited versions of the story aimed at a young audience have been matched by more child-focused illustrations, in particular in more recent times, but Chris Riddell has figuratively redeemed some of the spikier elements of the tale for a new audience. There are comic book versions of the story available, it has been filmed for television and Hanna-Barbera have produced a cartoon version of the voyages to Lilliput and Brobdingnag. P.J. Lynch has painted two scenes from *Gulliver's Travels*, bringing Gulliver back to a Lilliputian version of Cavan town in one.

It is a story which has inspired illustrators for over two centuries, but the full force of savagery of Swift's words, still relevant for our times, has yet to be captured in moving images. Meanwhile, the work of the artists discussed here can intrigue and delight the viewer with their own interpretations of this masterpiece of literature.

Read more ...

Humphrey Carpenter and Mari Prichard, *The Oxford Companion to Children's Literature*, Oxford, Oxford University Press, 1984.
S. Houfe, *The Dictionary of 19th Century British Book Illustrators and Charicaturists*, Wooodbridge, Suffolk, Antique Collector's Club, 1981.
Douglas Martin, *The Telling Line: essays on fifteen contemporary book illustrators*, London, Julia McRæ Books, 1989.

Editions discussed listed by name of illustrator. Except where the title differs from *Travels into Several Remote Nations of the World* or *Gulliver's Travels* it is not given.
Ambrus, Victor (1992). Adapted by James Riordan, Oxford, Oxford University Press.
Baltzer, Hans (1961). Edited by Elaine Moss, London, Constable Young Books Ltd.
Bawden, Edward (1948). London, Folio Society.
Browne, Gordon F. (1886). London, Blackie.
Bull, René (1928). Edited by F.J. Harvey Darton, London, Ward.
Grandville, J.J. (1838). With a new foreword by Denis Donoghue (1988), New York, Da Capo Press Inc.
Hargreaves, Martin (2000). London, Dorling Kindersley.
Hassall, John (1915). London, Blackie & Son.
Jackson, A.E. (1911). London, Ernest Nister.
Jacques, Robin (1955). Oxford, Oxford University Press.
Jones, David (1925). Waltham St. Lawrence, Berkshire, Golden Cockerel Press.
King, Alexander (1929). London, Limited Editions Club.
Lemke, Horst (1961) *Gullivers*

Reisen, nacherzählt von Erich Kästner. Zürich, Atrium-Verl.
Millar, James (1976). Belfast, Appletree Press.
Morten, Thomas (1865). London, Cassell, Petter & Galpin.
Mossa, R.G. (1938). London, Hodder & Stoughton.
Ovani, Germano (2002). Columbus, Ohio, McGraw-Hill Children's Publishing.
Pogány, Willy (1919). London, Harrap.
Poirson, V.A. (1886). London, Nimmo.
Prittie, Edwin John (1930). Philadelphia, J.C. Winston.
Rackham, Arthur (1899; 1909). London, Dent.
Rhead, Louis (1913). New York & London, Harper.
Riddell, Chris (2004). *Jonathan Swift's Gulliver*. Retold by Martin Jenkins. London, Walker Books. Spirin, Gennady (1993). *Gulliver's Adventures in Lilliput*. New York, Philomel Books.
Thomson, J.G. (1864). London, S.O. Beeton.
Whistler, Rex (1930). London, Cresset Press, reprinted by Herbert Press (1984).
Winter, Milo (1912). New York, Rand.

Chris Riddell

V

JONATHAN SWIFT'S Gulliver, 2004

Celia Keenan

Jonathan Swift's Gulliver retold by Martin Jenkins and illustrated by Chris Riddell is possibly the most ambitious retelling for children of Swift's classic. The extraordinary quality especially of its illustration has been widely recognised. It was awarded the Kate Greenaway Medal 2004 in Britain and the Parents' Choice Award, Gold 2005, Picture Books in the United States. Both Jenkins and Riddell would seem perfectly placed in terms of their experience, temperament and artistic skills to undertake this work. Martin Jenkins' own travels and work as a conservation biologist, and his track record as a writer of high-quality information books committed to raising awareness of environmental and conservation issues for children mean that he is uniquely qualified to re-tell Gulliver's story for children in the twenty-first century. Chris Riddell is a highly regarded creator of books for children, and an illustrator of other writers' work, best known perhaps for his collaboration with Paul Stewart in illustrating the Edge Chronicles series. He is also a very highly regarded award-winning political cartoonist for publications such as *The Observer, The New Statesman, The Independent.* In the early 1990s his cartoons were informed by a satirical anger reminiscent of Swift's and, like Swift's, directed at political corruption, because he felt that British society ' had a millenarian feeling of decay, a suppurating, pustular mood'.

Riddell illustrates the eleven by nine and a half inch sized book, richly and exuberantly with seventy water-colour plates, and many black-and-white line drawings mostly in comic cartoon style. The colour is very bright, attractive and stimulating and varies dramatically from one of the adventures to the next. The work contains two full double spreads, the first a map of Gulliver's travels at the very beginning, and the second a picture of Gulliver outstretched and pinned down by the Lilliputians when he first arrives in Lilliput. There are many single-page spreads and one and a half-page spreads that cross the gutter, along with quarter-page illustrations and small black and white insets within paragraphs. Certain motifs are cleverly repeated throughout. Taking his cue from the fact that the Lilliputians have had a religious-like civil war about eggs, Riddell uses a riot of comic/iconic images of birds and eggs as a signature to that entire adventure. Even the ships have bird figures for their mastheads. In addition Gulliver's blue Lilliputian coverlet/back-pack, decorated with vivid white and yellow eggs, accompanies him on his final journey in the land of the Houyhnhnms, creating visual continuity from the beginning to the end of the book. Riddell sometimes takes his cue from Swift's original rather than from Jenkins' retelling, as for example when he depicts the Brobdingnagians as wearing stereotypical oriental costume and using oriental utensils, obviously inspired by Swift's text where we are told their clothes 'resemble the Persian and Chinese'. Riddell, in an interview with Elspeth Hyams in 2005, states that there was no authorial brief, 'I am reacting to Martin's text'. Given that freedom, Riddell says 'The result was a big picture book, rather than a (possibly intimidating) "great big book"'. He did not want 'a reverential retelling', principally text and then an illustration, 'or a grand coffee-table book', but 'something very accessible, which invites you to be amused and endlessly entertained'. He also says that he was aiming at ' that picture-book sensibility, so kids pick it up and look at the pictures... not necessarily sequentially... Each spread is a little episode on its own that can be read almost on its own. It doesn't need to match the order of the book, you can dip in... I kept the colours very bright and the pace friendly so that you are not overwhelmed by detail.' His imagined reader of his pictures is somewhat younger than the target age. 'I was thinking of a child of six or seven picking it up and flicking through'. He also says he saw *Gulliver's Travels* as the ultimate shaggy dog story. He adds, significantly, that though Gulliver is likeable in some ways, 'he is also full of himself... by the time he is stranded with the horses his crew have got fed up with him. He's completely insufferable. I dressed him up in finery and lace and a frock-coat, to suggest he was pompous.' That latter comment is revealing because there is little in Swift's or Jenkins' texts to suggest that Gulliver has become more pompous.

Riddell's comments in this interview indicate that in his view there does not need to be a match between text and illustration: that images are not there to advance the narrative, but to amuse; that they need not be viewed sequentially. In essence what Riddell is doing is akin to certain features of jazz in music. He provides comic improvisations and variations on themes and images from Swift to accompany Jenkins' text. That means that the illustrations are not strictly in the service of the story.

All four books of Swift's original are substantially represented here. Although this version is not unique in giving all four sections (*Gulliver's Travels Adapted for the Young*, W.B. Scott, illustrated by A.E. Jackson, 1911, also gave all four books) the more usual retellings for children concentrate on the first two books only.

In Swift's original work his narrator, Gulliver, sustains his role convincingly because he is a plain man, a surgeon and sailor who takes the world more or less as he finds it, whose needs are simple and basic, who is not driven by curiosity or imagination or even by ambition but by a certain restlessness, a need to escape his wife and family. His prose is simple, and for much of the time, spare. The effect of that very plainness has been to convince readers that they are reading something close to the unadorned truth. In Charlotte Bronte's novel, *Jane Eyre*, (chapter 3) Jane, another rather plain narrator, recounts her childhood responses to Gulliver's story. It is likely that Jane has been reading a children's illustrated version, since she discusses only the first two books, those which were most frequently adapted for children. She mentions that she responded as if to a work of realism, seeing the landscape and animals and human figures as actual and Lilliput and Brobdingnag as countries she might visit some day. 'This book I had again and again perused with delight. I considered it a narrative of facts and discovered in it a vein of interest deeper than what I found in fairy tales'. Perhaps because Jane herself has just been through a major psychological crisis, she also now responds to the darker aspects of Swift's book, however, seeing Gulliver as, 'a most desolate wanderer in most dread and dangerous regions'.

Chris Riddell

Everything about the presentation of Swift's original work, whether the English edition of 1726 or the Irish edition of 1735, with its opening letter from Richard Sympson, Gulliver's 'cousin' and 'intimate friend', to the reader, is designed to enable the reader to suspend disbelief, to enter this as he or she would any travel book: to accept the reliability of Gulliver as narrator ('it became a sort of proverb among his neighbours in Redriff, when anyone affirmed a thing, to say it was as true as if Mr Gulliver had spoke it' *Writings of Swift*, p.viii).

The experience of first seeing and opening the Martin Jenkins/Chris Riddell version is precisely the opposite to opening Swift's original or indeed many of the retellings for children. From the highly comic, clown-like, motley-attired Gulliver that is depicted in a daring mock-crucifixion on the dust-jacket to the drunken leprechaun-like Gulliver on the fly-leaf, to the bespectacled Gulliver dressed in a mixture of clothing from all four lands of his travels on the title-page, to the insane Gulliver frantically perusing the scattered manuscript of his travels, secretly observed by his anxious wife, everything is visually designed to convince the reader that he or she is entering a world of absurd or comic fantasy and not a traditional travel book. In a post-modern way the book draws attention to itself as artefact. The book design, page layout, subversion of traditional page margins, variety of ways in which lists are compiled, movement of text around the illustrations all combine so that the reader cannot lose him- or her-self in the book. They also make the text difficult to read in the sense that the reader is constantly obliged to look up and down and back and forth across double spreads to follow the narrative, rather like reading a comic or graphic novel, but with much more text. The effect is radically different from encountering Swift's original work, or indeed from encountering most of the other illustrated versions for children, which by and large function in the tradition of realistic representational art. This difference is entirely created by the illustration and design. Jenkins' plain retelling is by and large faithful to both the tone and detail of Swift's original.

The Jenkins/Riddell version has a different emphasis in shape or structure to Swift's original. That original is a linear narrative beginning in chapter one, book one, with an account of Gulliver's history, continuing with sixteen years of travels and then five years at home in England completing the manuscript. The sense of linear and chronological continuity is not really disrupted by the accompanying letter from Gulliver to his supposed publisher, published in the 1735 edition, as the reader is most likely to read that after having read the main story beginning in book one chapter one. However that cannot happen in the Jenkins/Riddell version because the visual emphasis on the 'insane' Gulliver at the beginning and particularly the powerful illustrations mentioned already create a sense of circularity. There is the feeling that we begin with a comically insane Gulliver before the causes of his insanity are understood. In Swift's original Gulliver's madness is slowly and painstakingly constructed and developed over time and is seen as a logical response to the irrationality of man, in Swift's view wrongly defined as a rational animal, but in fact merely an animal 'capable of reason'. For that reason there is a sense that Swift's great satiric and moral purpose may be sidestepped in the Jenkins/Riddell version. One American reviewer, Preston Harper, expressed the view that 'the book needs an introduction that explains Swift's purpose in writing the book and perhaps some footnotes to explain the satire because the humorous pictures will probably leave the reader feeling the he has read a funny book whereas this is one of the darkest books in Western literature.'

Swift's Gulliver, as narrator, is the reader's guide. If the satire is to work, if the reader is to become aware of his or her own folly, some level of identification with Gulliver is essential. He is of course gullible but in spite of all his limitations he is a competent practical and resourceful figure. He can swim well, even fully clothed. He is a surgeon. He is a remarkable linguist who is already competent in a number of European languages before his travels begin. He learns the many languages of the lands he visits very quickly and well. He describes all

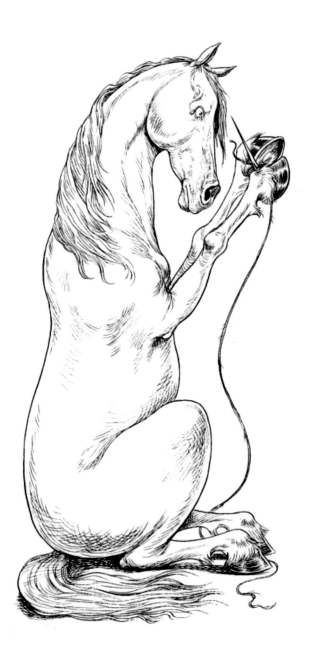

manner of physical sensation with precision. He makes clothes and furniture from unfamiliar materials. He builds a seaworthy boat. He converses with all manner of beings. He is merciful. He tries to behave politely and consider political necessities. He plays many roles to please those he depends on. He has some modest political principles, for example he rejects slavery and colonialism. He survives. As the book approaches the end his feelings are increasingly called into play until the reader is drawn into his shock and sorrow at being exiled from his beloved Houyhnhnms. All of these characteristics are faithfully preserved in the Jenkins text, but are for the most part subverted in the illustrations where most of the time Gulliver appears silly, as in the tradition of political cartoons.

Jenkins' retelling of book one, of Gulliver's arrival in Lilliput, of his finding himself tied down on the shore and of his first encounter with the Lilliputians is written economically, plainly, simply, very much in tune with the original but lacking the intensity of Swift's concentration on physical sensation. This section is comparatively longer than the other three sections, in contrast to Swift's original where it is shorter. The reader of Jenkins' text is invited to sympathise with Gulliver's physical pain and discomfort: 'I was instantly bombarded with hundreds of minute arrows which pricked me like so many needles and hurt terribly' (p.12). However the accompanying illustration, a stunning one and a half-page spread, makes such sympathy difficult, because it is riotously comic with, in particular, a single arrow sticking out of Gulliver's bulbous nose.

Jenkins captures the complexity of point-of view in Swift. Much of the time we see things through Gulliver's eyes but frequently Swift's most biting satire comes from other figures. Much of Swift's satire is included in the text, including the account of high-rope dancing by courtiers to win advancement, the conflict in Lilliput between courtiers who wear high-heeled and low-heeled shoes, and between Lilliput and Blefuscu - the war of Big Endians and Little Endians. Gulliver defeats the Blefuscu threat to Lilliput, but refuses to destroy

Chris Riddell

and facilitate the re-colonisation of Blefuscu, as he does not wish to play a part in turning a brave people into slaves. Jenkins keeps the anti-colonial message of Swift's original. There is treachery and small-mindedness in Lilliput and Gulliver reaches a new understanding of 'how treacherous courts and ministers could be'.

In the episode where Gulliver urinates on the empress's apartments to extinguish a fire the synergy between text and image is striking. The illustration, showing Gulliver's back, his head partially turned back revealing a single slightly scared eye against lurid flaming sky, the shocked empress, and the stunned birds is a wonderful comic gloss on the economy and restraint of the text (p.36, 37).

The sexual humour of the alleged affair between Gulliver and the treasurer's wife is preserved in Jenkins' version. 'It has been said that the treasurer's wife took something of a fancy to me and even visited me alone in secret' (p.40). In a number of tiny visual details, such as Gulliver's and the treasurer's wife's possession of each other's portrait, it is suggested that this comic unequal relationship is less innocent than Gulliver admits when he insists that when visiting him she was always chaperoned by her sister or daughter. It is above all in the Lilliput book that children's illustrators have traditionally exploited the possibilities of perspective, of proportionality, a response to which is implicit in the *Jane Eyre* quotation mentioned earlier. However because of the comic cartoon nature of Riddell's illustration there is very little continuous sense of perspective. There is instead a series of direct and varying contrasts between big and little.

In book two, the voyage to Brobdingnag, Jenkins' narrative again stays very close to Swift's. In Swift's original Gulliver frequently experiences the world as a child might do: finding himself dressed, fed, nursed, tended, petted, neglected and abused, by the giants in the arbitrary way that children are frequently treated by adults. Jenkins' narrative allows the reader to identify with Gulliver's powerlessness as it does with Gulliver's terror and courage when threatened by a series of giant animals that distinguish this book, ranging from the initial giant cat, through to the rat, spaniel, monkey, frog, and giant wasps until he is finally carried off and dropped by an eagle bringing this voyage to an end. Exploited and put on display for profit, Gulliver becomes ill and almost dies from exhaustion. His nurse and protector, indeed one of only two real friends in the book, is a nine-year-old child worker, Glumdalclitch. Swift's and Jenkins' texts reflect a world in which child labour and child-giftedness were widely exploited—think of Blake's child-victims, or even the juvenile career of Mozart. (In a very interesting essay, 'The Yahoo in the Doll's House, *Gulliver's Travels*: The Children's Classic', John Traugott, examining the first two books of Swift's work, argues that the child-like ludic quality of both books is central to Swift's project). Gulliver also reflects a childlike fascination with unpleasant or gross adult physicality, though in Jenkins' retelling, Swift's misogyny, his concentration on details of female anatomy to reflect physical revulsion, is considerably and understandably toned down given modern sensitivity with regard to gender. Gulliver realises that however brave he is, he will always appear amusing or comic to the giants; that whether one is a hero or clown is a matter of perspective. Jenkins captures the essentially anti-heroic theme of Swift's original. Gulliver engages with the King of Brobdingnag to explain British and European politics and wars. There is a considerably shortened and restrained version of the anti-war section of Swift's writing in this chapter.

Book three of Swift's work, the voyage to Laputa, Balnibarbi, Luggnagg, Glubbdubdrib and Japan is the most disparate and least focused of Swift's narratives, and that most frequently omitted from children's retellings. Its plot seems loose. There is no companion character such as the King or Queen or Glumdalclitch in Brobdingnag, or the Master in the final book with whom Gulliver's thoughts and feelings are debated and tested. It is not surprising that Jenkins and Riddell reproduce much of it however because it has a strong surreal science fiction element which has a particularly modern appeal. Some of its details seem particularly relevant in the 21st-century world in which scientists have cloned a sheep, made a mouse grow a human ear, and where people have

their bodies frozen in the hope of defeating mortality. The rulers and inhabitants of the various countries visited are, for the most part, humans of normal size, though of decidedly odd characteristics and mentalities. The section ends with an actual visit to Japan. The humorous name of the island of Laputa (possibly Spanish for a whore) has serendipitous evocations for the modern reader, with its suggestion of 'laptop' and 'computer', so appropriate in a world in which the only subjects studied are mathematics and music, and in which a prototype computer exists in the form of a machine to enable people to write books on topics they know nothing about. Much of Swift's satire is directed at 'The Royal Society of London for The Improvement of Knowledge'. Swift's original work here must be one of the greatest anti-intellectual works of literature, raging as it does against everything progressive in enlightenment thought. It is in that sense a work of radical conservatism. It contains a satiric attack on enlightenment philosophy, science, linguistics, medicine, music, mathematics, history, and politics. Intellectuals are stereotyped as distracted, inattentive, forgetful, and ineffective creatures. Their projects are ridiculous, even obscene. Mathematicians cannot measure correctly to make a suit for Gulliver. Musicologists create only cacophony. Architects build houses that cannot function. Scientific projects reach a nadir as one scientist attempts to reconvert excrement into food. In Balnibarbi sensible agriculture is destroyed by ideas and ideology. In Glubbdubdrib, the land of sorcerers, the ghost of the Greek philosopher Aristotle dismisses the work of enlightenment philosopher Descartes. Newton's theory of gravity is dismissed as mere fashion that will become outdated. Jenkins keeps all these references as well as those to historical figures such as Alexander the Great, Julius Cæsar and Thomas More. It is interesting to speculate on the challenge of this to the modern child reader. It is difficult to imagine that those of the target age of between nine and twelve would engage meaningfully with much of it, without detailed explanation. They would however thoroughly enjoy the richness, inventiveness, humour, absurdity, and scatological rudeness of the illustration.

Chris Riddell

In fact it seems to me that the illustration in this section is the most successful in the whole work, capturing the almost insane energy of the original.

The anti-colonial politics of Swift is replicated as well: Laputa, the flying island, overcomes rebellion in its dependant territories by hovering over them and blocking out sunlight and rain. Swift's anti-Dutch and anti-Japanese comments, which have a religious basis, are omitted from this version. This section ends with a single-page spread in black and white depicting a romantic embrace between Gulliver and his wife on his arrival home, which links in beautifully with the opening of the final section where a parallel page and a half spread shows Gulliver blithely riding away from his now pregnant wife.

Book four represents the increasing darkness of Swift's vision. Jenkins retains all the important episodes and details of Swift's narrative: Gulliver's shock and disgust in his encounters with the simian Yahoos, his seduction by the quiet dignity and rationality of the Houyhnhnms, his alienation from humanity and his descent into loneliness and madness. Both Yahoos and Houyhnhnms are superbly and realistically drawn and coloured by Riddell. There is something very expressive about both creatures. Gulliver becomes like a child again here, first drinking a bowl of milk, then listening and learning carefully. The Houyhnhnms have no word for lying: instead they use the awkward phrase 'he said the thing which is not.' Neither Houyhnhnms nor Yahoos share the human preoccupation with clothes. Gulliver is exposed here and obliged to show his almost naked body. The Houyhnhnms cannot understand his shame about private parts of the body. Gulliver's master cannot understand 'why nature should teach us to hide anything that nature has given us' (p.126).

In conversations between Gulliver and his master the anti-war theme reaches a terrifying climax in Swift's original that continues over several pages: saying that over a million people have been killed in the recent long war with France: listing the causes of war, including a savage account of weapons and the destruction they cause and ending with ... 'beheld the dead bodies drop down from the clouds to the great diversion of all spectators' (*Writings of Swift*, p.214). The culmination of this account is one of shock and silence, 'My master commanded me silence.' In the Jenkins/Riddell version it is much more briefly rendered. The section is stronger and more forthright in conveying Swift's attack on political corruption. On p.130-31 there is a superb sepia-tinted centre page illustration suggesting greed, luxury, lust, and disease, presided over by a figure of death in a brown habit in the top-left corner. This is an image that refuses to condescend or patronise its young reader. This section discretely reflects Swift's misogyny in its depiction of a female Yahoo who is attracted to Gulliver and pounces on him. Jenkins' text is reticent about her intentions and desires: 'Once when I was bathing I was leapt on by a young female Yahoo. Goodness knows what would have happened if the sorrel nag, who was close by and keeping a watch on me, had not chased it off'. However, Riddell's illustration, though still discrete, conveys a decidedly comic sexual rapaciousness in the widely open mouth and eyes of the Yahoo (p.134-35).

Gulliver finds that he is happy in the company of the Houyhnhnms. His devastation at his rejection by the Houyhnhnms is total. In Jenkins' prose, which is close to Swift's, the poetry of the sorrel nag's valedictory 'Hnuy illa nyha maja, Yahoo, Take care of yourself, gentle Yahoo' (p.138) is perfectly matched by Riddell's accompanying beautiful full-page seascape which captures the sorrow and despair of Gulliver. Gulliver, a sad, grey, helpless slumped figure, bent almost double in despair sits in the little boat that he has built himself, surrounded by enormous dark blue-green waves tipped with white, reminiscent of the work of Hokusai, under a cloudy and stormy sky (p.139). There is an epilogue on the folly of the colonial enterprise explaining why Gulliver does not claim the Houyhnhnm's lands for the king, in white print on black background echoing the introduction, set in the same room, but this time the manuscript has become a book which is read with close attention by Gulliver's serious-looking young son, at the same table with the same candle. The effect is sober, even sad: a fitting end.

Chris Riddell

Most of Swift's major thematic concerns and the objects of his satire are represented in Jenkins' text and in Riddell's illustration. These include his concern with education, intellectual satire, his political satire, and in gentler forms his religious satire, his misogynistic comments, his obsession with the body, attack on colonialism and his ultimate attack on human pride. Possibly Swift's most striking theme is his consistent attack on war: the silliness of its causes, the monstrous nature of its weaponry, the horror and cruelty of its results. There is a clear anti-war section in three out of the four books, and the horror and revulsion grow in intensity from one book to the next. However this theme, though treated in each section of the Jenkins/Riddell version, is given surprisingly little force or prominence and, given the scale of the illustration in the book as a whole, is very modestly illustrated. This reticence is especially puzzling in view of the fact that the book was published a year after the 2003 invasion of Iraq, the build-up to which had provoked the most sustained and popular anti-war protest in British history. In Jenkins' and Riddell's account these sections are considerably shortened and simplified. In the Brobdingnag section Jenkins's account of war is one paragraph long and retains little of Swift's terrible brutality. The only accompanying illustration is one of Gulliver and the king in conversation (p.70-71). The reader is expected to register the full horror of what has been described from the expression depicted on the king's partial side-face. In the final book where Gulliver again gives his master an account of war, Riddell's illustration consists of a single, relatively small, pink-coloured image of the dead on a battlefield at the end of action, observed by a bemused rider-less horse (p.128-29). It has little of the power of, for example Raymond Briggs' great anti-war battle scenes in *The Tin Pot General and the Old Iron Woman*, or indeed in Michæl Foreman's *War-Game*. Though it may be argued that, in a book for the young, accounts of violence need to be toned down, there are strong precedents for realistic and hard-hitting anti-war illustration in British picturebooks. One of the most recognisable contemporarily relevant enduring universal themes in

116

Swift is his consistent anti-war stance. It seems a pity not to highlight this in what promises to be a definitive version for children in the 21st century. That failure may relate to the overall comic intention of the illustrator as discussed earlier. Though Jenkins re-tells Swift's story with care, fidelity and fine writing, and though Riddell illustrates it superbly, wittily, and generously, and with a great variety of styles, the essence of Swift's satire eludes them.

Read more...

On Swift:

Irvin Ehrenpreis, *Swift: the man, his works, and the age,* 3 volumes, London, Methuen, 1962-1983.

David Nokes, *Jonathan Swift: a hypocrite reversed. A critical biography*, Oxford, Oxford University Press, 1985 (A good one volume biography).

Robert A. Greenberg and William B. Piper, editors, *The Writings of Jonathan Swift*. A Norton critical edition, New York, Norton, 1973 (references in the essay are to this edition of *Gulliver's Travels*).

Christopher Fox, editor, *The Cambridge Guide to Jonathan Swift*, Cambridge, Cambridge University Press, 2003.

John Traugott, 'The Yahoo in the Doll's House: *Gulliver's Travels* the Children's Classic' in Claude Rawson, editor, *English Satire and the Satiric Tradition*, Oxford, Basil Blackwell, 1984.

Mary Shine Thompson, 'Gulliver's Travels in the Land of Childhood' in Mary Shine Thompson and A.J. Piesse, editors, *Young Irelands: Studies in children's literature*, Dublin, Four Courts Press, 2008, (forthcoming).

On the work of Chris Riddell:

The British Cartoon Archive, University of Kent, http://opal.kent.ac.cartoonx-cgi/artist.py?id=143

CILIP 'From Fantasy to Satire: Elspeth Hyams talks to Chris Riddell',

http://www.cilip.org.uk/publications/updatemagazine/archive/archive2005/december/interviewwithchrisriddell.htm

http://www.imagesofdelight.com/client.asp?id=75

http://www//clcd/cgi_bin/member/search/f?./temp/~1fb06j:1

VI

Dublin City Public Libraries' SWIFT Collection

Máire Kennedy

Voyages de Gulliver 1813

VOYAGES
DE
GULLIVER,
TRADUITS DE L'ANGLAIS, DE SWIFT,
Par l'Abbé DES FONTAINES.
Edition ornée de douze Gravures.
TOME PREMIER.

A PARIS,
Chez GENETS jeune, Libraire, Rue Dauphine, N.° 14.
1813.

Jonathan Swift, Dean of St. Patrick's Cathedral, was born in Dublin in 1667, and died there 78 years later in 1745. Of English parentage, his birthplace was in Hoey's Court, a small square of tall seventeenth-century houses in the Dutch style, behind Werburgh Street, not far from St. Patrick's, where he served for over forty years, first as prebendary and then as dean. Although a reluctant Dubliner he is cherished by the people of the city and is considered one of Dublin's most eminent sons. In his day he was a well-known wit, renowned in high society, but his witticisms and sayings penetrated to the ordinary people and they were celebrated in song and story. These stories and ballads associated with 'the Dane' (Dean) have lived on in Irish folklore. He was a friend to the poor of the city, giving much of his income for charitable purposes and leaving money in his will to found St. Patrick's Hospital for Imbeciles, opened in 1757.

Swift's writings occupy a central place in the holdings of Dublin City Libraries, ranging from his political works, prose, satires, verse and sermons to his collected works in many editions. Early editions of these works in English and in translation were collected by Sir John T. Gilbert during the nineteenth century and his important library was purchased for the city in 1900. Early editions continue to be collected today, new editions, often augmented by critical notes, verse, and prose works in illustrated editions, are actively sought. Foreign language editions of Swift's works also find a place in the holdings, from early editions to recent translations. This area is currently being expanded to encourage research. Swift holdings have been acquired by donation and purchase since the setting up of the public library service in Dublin city in 1884. Modern editions of Swift's works are available for lending through the branch library network and editions of *Gulliver's Travels* for adults and children are purchased as they are published.

Dublin City Library and Archive in Pearse Street holds early editions of Swift's works, including political tracts published in London, and pamphlets concerning Irish affairs published in Dublin in the first decades of the eighteenth century. Dublin editions were originally issued by the printers John Harding, his widow Sarah Harding, and Thomas Hume. Swift involved himself in the controversy surrounding Wood's halfpence. His *Letters*, signed M. B., Drapier, were written in opposition to

William Wood's patent to mint this copper coinage for use in Ireland. His pamphlets, however, went beyond the immediate issue and made claims that Ireland had a right to make its own laws. A proclamation was issued against the anonymous author, and the printer of the pamphlets, John Harding, was arrested and jailed, he died in prison in April 1725. Swift's role in the Wood's halfpence controversy earned him the contemporary title 'Hibernian patriot' and the freedom of the city of Dublin. The original editions of the "Drapier's letters", printed by Harding in 1724, are in the Gilbert Library as well as a collected edition of all the letters issued the following year by George Faulkner. Several of these pamphlets were originally collected by the Newenham family of Belcamp Hall in Coolock and form part of the Newenham Pamphlets, purchased by John Gilbert in 1884.

The printer and bookseller, George Faulkner, became Swift's Dublin printer about 1729, receiving printing rights to many of his works, and publishing some of Swift's journalistic pieces in his newspaper *Faulkner's Dublin Journal*. Faulkner continued in his capacity as Swift's publisher until his own death in 1775. He was instrumental in collecting Swift's works and making them available to the reading public. A collected edition of works in four volumes, printed on fine Genoa paper, was published by subscription by Faulkner in 1735. The publication was supervised by Swift and textual errors were corrected. Faulkner's role was critical in identifying some lesser-known pieces written anonymously by Swift. Were it not for his collected edition published in Swift's lifetime, and with his co-operation, some of these items might not have survived, or might not now be attributable to Swift. Faulkner published a more extensive collected edition in 1763, the first posthumous *Works*, for which he gathered up a wide range of material from Swift's friends. Several editions of *Collected Works* have a place in the collections in fine Dublin bindings of the eighteenth and nineteenth centuries. Examples include the eleven volume *Works* published by Faulkner in 1763, bound in a lovely Dublin binding of contemporary sprinkled calf with a wide gilt border on the covers, spine decorated in gilt and all edges gilt; a 20 volume collected edition, printed by Faulkner in 1772, bound in contemporary

Plate.I Part.I *Page* 1.

Hogs I.

P Mintaon
I Good Fortune

I Naſſow

SUNDA

Sillabar

SUMATRA

Straits *of* Sunda

Metulei

Blefuſcu

Lilliput.

Mendendo

Diſcovered, A.D.1699.

Dimel

First edition 1726

Dublin edition 1727

Voyages de Gulliver 1730

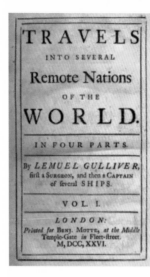

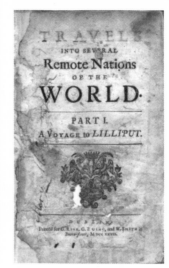

Le Nouveau Gulliver

Swift Hospital 1733

Drapier's Letter 1724

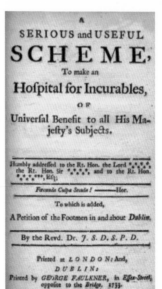

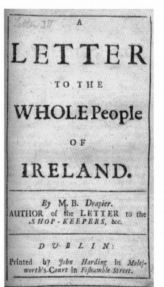

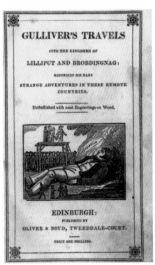

tree calf with gilt spines; and a 15 volume set printed for James Williams in 1774, bound in full contemporary calf with gilt decorated spines. A 24 volume set in the miniscule octodecimo (18mo) format, published in London from 1765 to 1775 contains copperplate illustrations. Gilbert held another set of *The Works of Jonathan Swift* in eleven volumes, with two additional volumes, published by Faulkner in 1763-65, and a 19 volume set of *The Works*, with notes and a life of the author by Sir Walter Scott, published in Edinburgh in 1824.

Travels into Several Remote Nations of the World. By Lemuel Gulliver, first a surgeon, and then a captain of several ships, to give the book its full title, was first published anonymously in London in October 1726. It found an immediate audience both for its savage political and social satire and for its imaginative narratives, making it a favourite among readers. The first printing of *Gulliver's Travels* sold out in a very short time and two further printings were issued in the same year. Critical notes and keys to the different voyages made their appearance in London shortly after publication, with Dean Swift identified as the author on

the title pages. Three Dublin editions were published immediately, the first in late 1726, containing some of Swift's corrections to the first London edition, printed by and for John Hyde, printer and bookseller in Dame Street. The next issue was printed for George Risk, George Ewing and William Smith, booksellers in Dame Street; it was advertised in December 1726, but its imprint gives the date 1727. The third is a reprint of the second edition, printed for George Risk, George Ewing and William Smith, and dated 1727. The printer is S.P., who may be Sylvanus Pepyat, bookseller and stationer to the city, or more likely Deborah Powell, printer, widow of Stephen Powell, printing in the name of her under-age son, Samuel. Irish editions are now very scarce and hard to acquire. Trinity College Dublin holds a copy of the second Dublin edition, the National Library of Ireland holds two copies of the Dublin edition of 1727, and a portion of that same edition, containing parts I and II only, was collected by the bibliographer E.R. McClintock Dix and donated to Dublin City Libraries. Swift made several corrections to *Gulliver's Travels* before its publication by Faulkner in 1735. Writing to Faulkner he observed:

'Since you intend to print a new edition of that book, I must tell you that the English printer made several alterations which I much disapprove of'. The edition published by Faulkner as volume three of *The Works* in 1735 is considered the most correct, and in the publisher's words 'it may be truly said, a genuine and correct edition of this author's works was never publish'd till this time'.

Swift's friends and correspondents John Gay and Alexander Pope wrote to him soon after publication of *Gulliver's Travels* (16 and 17 November 1726), congratulating him on his wonderful book. Gay wrote: 'From the highest to the lowest it is universally read, from the cabinet-council to the nursery'. Therefore, child readers were engaged with the story from the start. Abridged versions made their appearance, appealing to children and to those with poor literacy skills, and costing less than the original two-volume version. In the intervening period of nearly 300 years the story has been abridged and retold countless times, editors concentrating on the fantasy and comic elements and omitting much of the political satire and some of the scenes considered offensive, or unsuitable

J.G. Thomson
Ballad singers

for young minds. Chapbook versions, sketching the bare outlines of the story, were published from the late eighteenth century. Versions retold especially for children usually confined themselves to the first two parts, the voyages to Lilliput and Brobdingnag.

The first edition had as its frontispiece an engraved portrait of the fictional author, Captain Lemuel Gulliver, in an oval frame. Two issues of the first edition are distinguished by the portrait frontispiece. In the A edition Gulliver's name is inscribed on a tablet under the oval, while in the B edition his name is inscribed around the oval, and the tablet contains a Latin inscription. Dublin City Libraries has the two volume set of the first edition with the B portrait. The four parts were illustrated with imaginary maps of each land, showing their supposed locations in relation to known places, such as Sumatra and Dimens Land (Van Diemen's Land) for Lilliput, the west coast of North America for Brobdingnag, Japan for Laputa and Lagado, and Lewins Land, New Holland (Australia) for Houyhnhnms Land. This gave credence to what set itself up as a journal of discovery to new lands, with the author giving an account

of the customs and manners of the inhabitants. Later illustrated editions often omitted the maps. Late eighteenth- and early nineteenth-century editions carried engraved images of selected scenes from the travels: fine copperplates in expensive editions and poorer quality woodcuts in cheap editions. A French language edition from the collections, published in Paris in 1813, is illustrated with high quality wood engravings. One abridged version from the 1820s, published in Edinburgh, shows an engraving of the colossal Gulliver astride the Lilliputian capital as its frontispiece. Fine black and white engravings by Thomas Morten illustrate an edition from 1864-65, which was much reprinted during the nineteenth century. Improved technology allowed illustration to develop and by the mid-nineteenth century colour plates began to adorn the more up-market editions of the book. As colour printing became more affordable artists were given a freer rein to use their imaginations to interpret the many striking scenes from the travels. A full colour illustrated version from 1874, edited by Peter Pindar Junior, depicts scenes from Lilliput and Brobdingnag, with full colour plates and black and white drawings, styling itself an 'illustrated edition for the rising generation'.

Eighteenth- and early nineteenth-century illustrators of Gulliver remained anonymous; this was the custom before well-known artists turned their attention to illustrating books. The challenge to illustrate the travels began to be taken up by established artists and book illustrators over the last century and a half, resulting in a significant range of images spanning various artistic styles and fashions, some becoming iconic. No one illustrator is associated with *Gulliver's Travels*, readers have their own favourites, often based on childhood reading. Illustrated retellings designed for the entertainment of children are among the most memorable in literature. Artists from many countries have brought their particular visions to the travels and new insights can be gleaned from the varying interpretations. An edition published in 1864 with designs by J.G. Thomson, engraved by W.L. Thomas, robustly depicts key scenes from the book. V.A. Poirson's charming illustrations with colour wash, originally published in French editions, were published in English in 1886. Not all illustrated editions are geared towards children, many are specifically

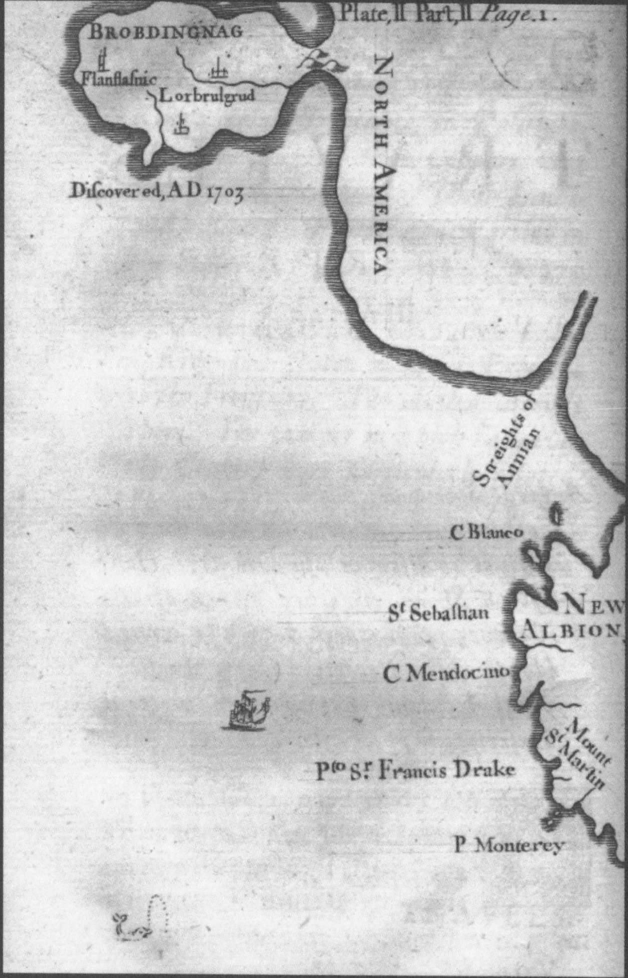

BROBDINGNAG

Flanflafnic

Lorbrulgrud

Difcovered, AD 1703

NORTH AMERICA

Streights of Annian

C Blanco

St Sebaftian

C Mendocino

NEW ALBION

Pto St Francis Drake

Mount St Martin

P Monterey

aimed at adults, examples include Alexander King's 1929 edition from The Limited Editions Club; Rex Whistler's edition first published in 1930 and reissued in 1984; the collectors' edition from the Folio Society with full-page colour lithographs by Edward Bawden, published in 1948; and most recently Chris Riddell's 2004 edition, with an appeal for adults and children alike, discussed in Celia Keenan's chapter in this volume. Several of these illustrated editions have been acquired for Dublin city's collections and are available for research. For a fuller discussion of some of the more noteworthy illustrators see Valerie Coghlan's chapter 'Picturing Gulliver'.

Gulliver's Travels has been translated into scores of languages. The speed with which new translations followed the original publication is noteworthy, some just months after the first edition was published. French and Dutch translations made their appearance in January 1727, published in The Hague, and a French translation was published in Paris in March 1727. The first German translation appeared in Hamburg in 1727, and the first Italian translation was published in Venice in 1729. Other translations into European languages continued throughout the eighteenth century, making it an international best-seller. A copy of *Voyages du Capitaine Lemuel Gulliver en Divers Pays Eloignez*, published in The Hague in 1730, was purchased by John Gilbert.

The imaginative influence of the book became apparent quickly. A sequel was written in French by the Abbé Pierre-François Guyot Desfontaines in 1730: *Le Nouveau Gulliver, ou Voyage de Jean Gulliver, Fils du Capitaine Gulliver, traduit d'un manuscrit anglois par Monsieur L.D.F.* It purported to describe a voyage undertaken by Lemuel Gulliver's son, John. The Abbé Desfontaines was a correspondent of Swift's and he translated the original work into French; many eighteenth-century French editions contain the sequel as the final part of the *Travels*. Two early French editions are available in the Dublin city collections, the first edition in two volumes, published in Paris in 1730 and an engraved edition in four volumes published in Paris in 1813. The first two volumes of the 1813 edition contain Swift's Gulliver while volumes three and four contain Desfontaines' sequel. This sequel had a contemporary popularity and was translated into other languages in the 1730s, including English, Dutch and German. A Portuguese edition in three volumes was published in Lisbon in 1804, the first two volumes of which are held by Dublin City Libraries as part of its wider collection of Swift-associated holdings.

Swift's own wide reading influenced his writing. As a 'graduate and a gentleman' he had access to Ireland's first public library, Archbishop Marsh's Library, adjacent to St. Patrick's, which was founded in 1701. Here he could read religious treatises, works by classical authors, works of travel and history, and pore over the wonderful folio maps in the library. In his own private library also he had a good collection of serious and entertaining reading matter. After his death in 1745 his library was sold by auction and a printed catalogue issued. He read the works of contemporary authors, numbering among his friends the playwright John Gay, the satirist John Arbuthnot and the poet Alexander Pope. He corresponded with the Abbé Desfontaines and Voltaire in French. Swift helped to raise subscriptions in Ireland for Voltaire's new work, *La Henriade*, when it was published in London in 1728, and he held a copy in his own library. In his library he had many travel books, including a copy of Joseph Addison's *Travels Through Italy* (London, 1705), presented to him by the author; books of travels to America, *Voyages and Discoveries in South America* (London, 1698) and *Wafer's Voyage to the Isthmus of America* (London, 1699); and a late sixteenth-century travel book, Richard Hakluyt's *Collection of Voyages of the English Nation*. These narratives served him well when he came to write his own account of travels to strange and wonderful lands. Curiously, he did not have a copy of Daniel Defoe's *Robinson Crusoe*, published in 1719, but he may have read it from the library of one of his friends.

Dublin City Libraries aim to hold as comprehensive a collection as possible of Swift's works for research and to promote the pleasure of reading his timeless writings. Works of criticism and interpretation and works associated with Swift are also acquired. New acquisitions are made each year to expand and develop the holdings. Sister institutions in the city, Trinity College library, National Library of Ireland, Archbishop Marsh's Library and the library of The Royal Irish Academy hold extensive Swift collections, and no appreciation of Swift's works is complete without visiting the holdings of each library.

Read more ...

http://www.dublincity.ie/living_in_the_city/libraries/ for Dublin City Public Libraries' online catalogue.

A Bibliography of the Writings of Jonathan Swift, second edition, revised and corrected by Dr. H. Teerink, edited by Arthur H. Scouten, Philadelphia, University of Pennsylvania Press, 1963.

The Correspondence of Jonathan Swift, edited by Harold Williams, 5 volumes, Oxford, Clarendon Press, 1963-72.

Prince of Dublin Printers: the letters of George Faulkner, edited by Robert E. Ward, Lexington, The University Press of Kentucky, 1972.

Joseph McMinn, 'Printing Swift', Éire-Ireland, XX, no. 1 (1985), pp. 143-49.

Harold Williams, Dean Swift's Library, with a facsimile of the original sale catalogue, Cambridge, at the University Press, 1932.

A Catalogue of Books, the Library of the late Rev. Dr. Swift, Dean of St. Patrick's, Dublin. To be sold by auction, Dublin, printed for George Faulkner, in Essex-Street, 1745.

Muriel McCarthy, All Graduates and Gentlemen: Marsh's Library, Dublin, O'Brien Press, 1980.

VII

The Influence of JONATHAN SWIFT on Anglo-Irish Writing

Eibhlín Evans

The early period of effective abandonment by his immediate family left Swift with a permanent sense of being alone.

Swift·has·left·us¶

Alongside the ever popular *Gulliver's Travels* his most celebrated works,

150·or·so·prose·works,¶

in terms of Anglo-Irish writing, are *A Tale of a Tub* (1704),

280·pœms¶

The Battle of the Books (1697), *The Drapier's Letters* (1724) and *A Modest Proposal* (1729).

and·over·700·letters.#

While Swift tried hard to pass off his most famous work, *Gulliver's Travels* (1726), as the autobiographical writing of one Lemuel Gulliver those who knew him quickly identified Swift as the author. Since then Swift and Gulliver have become inseparable and his fame is due, in many quarters, to this text alone. Few readers, especially outside Ireland, are aware of Swift's other masterpieces and even fewer are alert to his important influence on Anglo-Irish writing. If, like Gulliver, we travel beyond the shores of Swift's singular 'novel' we find a range of writing duly celebrated for its innovation and most of all, for its inventive satire, its powerful insights, and in some cases, its political influence.

We also find in Swift's writing an influential literary model adopted and adapted very successfully by successive generations of Anglo-Irish writers and this essay will highlight Swift's literary legacy and will explore how it is registered in subsequent classics, including the writing of Maria Edgeworth, George Bernard Shaw, James Joyce and Flann O'Brien.

Swift was master of the political and philosophical satire, a prolific poet and essayist, a travel writer, a novelist and, through *Gulliver's Travels,* he is also considered a children's author. While his *œuvre* embraces many literary forms one of the most striking features of Swift's writing is its blending of literary genres within individual texts. However, it must be remembered that literature in the eighteenth century was not divided into distinct genres. Poetic writing was, of course, recognised as a separate literary form but prose was not always segregated into categories. During Swift's lifetime fiction was in its infancy and the novel did not exist in the way we understand it in its modern form. Its subsequent division into romance, thriller, mystery writing (or one of the many other sub-categories we now recognise) was not yet established. Travel writing too, for obvious reasons, was an expanding arena. Writers in the eighteenth century were not constrained by our current conventions and, even had they existed, it is doubtful that Swift would have observed them anyway.

Swift's multi-generic freedoms did, however, bequeath a rich panoply of literary forms to his Anglo-Irish successors. Writers could select from a range of skilled achievements within individual literary forms while others could find inspiration within his multi-generic approach. However, Swift and satire have become synonymous and it is no surprise to find his legacy most pronounced in the work of those who seek to comment on the Anglo-Irish situation in a less than favourable fashion via this form of writing.

Swift has left us 150 or so prose works, 280 poems and over 800 letters. Alongside the ever popular *Gulliver's Travels* his most celebrated works, in terms of Anglo-Irish writing, are *A Tale of a Tub* (1704), *The Battle of the Books* (1697), *The Drapier's Letters* (1724) and *A Modest Proposal* (1729). The latter two texts were historically and economically significant in Irish history and Swift's reputation as a heroic figure rests on the political success achieved through their publication. In all Swift's 'Irish' publications we find humour, satire and biting critiques of the prevailing thought systems and, more importantly, of Swift's immediate political and historical struggles. These two are connected – that is philosophy and politics, and this is the genius of Swift's writing – the original marriage of morality and pressing political and social matters. Swift could qualify as the first Anglo-Irish writer, as Declan Kiberd puts it, (in relation to much later writing, but appropriate here nonetheless) to find the Irish colonial situation 'desperately interesting and interestingly desperate'.

'The Dane', (the Hiberno-English pronunciation of 'The Dean') as he was known, became the subject of many anecdotes, told in both English and Irish during his lifetime and for many years following his death. Although his racial identity and religious affiliation as a Church of Ireland cleric set him apart from the native population, his robust character, bawdy conversation and his outspoken criticism of his own community's mismanagement of Ireland endeared him to the Irish and he was hailed as a supporter if not a champion of their plight. Many stories of his wit and sagacity were circulated in the form of 'Jack Tales' and are still recounted today.

Apart from these it is important to know something of Swift's history and of the historical context of his writing before we can assess his influence. Jonathan Swift was born in Dublin, in the parish of St. Werburgh's in 1667. His father died before he was born; his mother returned to England to live shortly after his birth, leaving the hapless infant in the hands of a besotted nursemaid who soon afterwards kidnapped him and removed him to Whitehaven in England. Approximately two years later she and the infant returned to Dublin and resumed a more mundane existence. Swift was educated at Kilkenny School, and later at Trinity College, Dublin. On graduating in 1689 he moved to More Park, in Surrey, to become secretary to the celebrated writer and diplomat, Sir William Temple. Swift was to spend almost twenty four years moving back and forth between Ireland and England before taking up his post as Dean of St. Patrick's Cathedral in Dublin in 1713.

The early period of effective abandonment by his immediate family left Swift with a permanent sense of being alone. He was a member of the Anglo-Irish Protestant class, at that time a minority of approximately one-fifth of the island's population. His nomadic life left him with a degree of ambivalence towards both countries and a profound sense of belonging to neither. Yet he grew to be one of the most outspoken critics of the desperate situation of the native Irish and to be a passionate adversary of the ruling Anglo-Irish elite whose neglect of their responsibilities he abhorred.

While the relationship between Ireland and England is, historically, one of colonial domination of the former by the latter, critics have taken pains to differentiate this relationship as a unique colonial experience, where the distinctions between oppressor and oppressed are complex and nuanced – where a straightforward dichotomy of identities is never fully stable. Factors of proximity to the main territory of the coloniser; a shared language (eventually) and shared religious culture (Christianity), as well as levels of cultural assimilation and identification with the native people by those sent to rule the territory – and latterly the reverse where, post-independence writers have found a form of cultural colonialism difficult to defeat - all of these factors demand a different account of the relationship between the two parties involved. Jonathan Swift is a good example of the ambivalences that individuals caught up in such a situation were prey to and all of those Anglo-Irish writers most influenced by his writing share this duality and this ambivalent relationship to Ireland.

Swift's sympathies were never predictable along racial or religious lines. Ostensibly a member of the ruling Anglo-Irish class, he made it the target of his biting political assaults. As he matured he became a radical critic of power elites, demonstrating as Declan Kiberd points out, both an identity as a frustrated loyalist and as a fledgling nationalist. Over the body of his writing Swift displays a homelessness of mind – one that provided him with a viewpoint as 'Other', as outsider, and this is the origin of the anthropological tenor of much of his writing and the source of his incisive judgments and his often astute insights. This too is a feature of the personal profiles of all of those Anglo-Irish writers most influenced by Swift, Edgeworth, Shaw, Joyce and O'Brien all share this sense of apartness from their respective communities, in most cases sharing a sense of a conflicted identity.

The contradictions and ambivalences of Swift's personality are not confined to his political allegiances but are there also in other aspects of his profile. As a Church of Ireland clergyman of rank Swift's writing could be considered blasphemous and often included scatological material. Several of his biographers have indicted Swift on issues of his own moral conduct in relation to the women in his life, his companion Stella (Esther Johnson) and his alleged mistress, Vanessa (Esther Van Homrigh). He is a writer for

It·must·be¶

Swift shared Temple's belief that all historical enquiry

'alive·and·breathing'¶

reverts to questions of moral philosophy.

Swiſt·demanded,¶

History here is not factual lists of dates, events and personages,

imbued·with¶

related dryly in academic treatises.

insight·and·passion.#

whom many readers retain an ambivalent attitude, admiring his passion and his power of language while despairing of his misogyny and his class prejudices. None, however, doubt his power as a satirist, nor his important influence on his successors.

What Swift bequeathed to future generations of Irish writers was not the concern to centralise the plight of Ireland itself, as this would prove an inevitable preoccupation as the country suffered continually throughout the following centuries, but his legacy is most pronounced in the continued employment of a literary strategy which allowed Anglo-Irish writers to articulate their ongoing predicaments in powerful and innovative ways. Swift emerged from his long apprenticeship with Sir William Temple sharing two central beliefs with his former master. The first is the conviction that human nature, over space and time, is fundamentally the same imperfect entity and, secondly, that the true end point of the study of history and the true examination of historical episodes is a form of moral philosophy. Swift shared Temple's belief that all historical enquiry reverts to questions of moral philosophy. History here is not factual lists of dates, events and personages, related dryly in academic treatises. It must be 'alive and breathing' Swift demanded, imbued with insight and passion. But most importantly, historical events have a moral dimension that needs to be examined and contemporary historical moments deserve to be subjected to moral questioning.

Swift's experience of imperfect humanity and his immediate experience of history in the making in the disputes and debates raging around him led him to adopt a literary strategy in line with his beliefs. This strategy depended on a literary doubleness in Swift's writing where the surface narrative is always shadowed by a playful, satirical, sometimes devious, often anarchic double. This is not just an undertow of biting, witty irreverence, at once comic and serious, sometimes tinged with horror, but a powerful tool that undermines, and in many cases eventually yields, an overwhelming assault on the original testimony. The easy urbanity of his mentor Sir William Temple is aped in the surface smoothness of the writing. This is then undercut and sabotaged by the extremes of the examples offered and ultimately by the absurdity of the conclusions that are allowed to follow. *A Tale of a Tub* includes this strategy with Swift's de-bunking of both the ancient Herodotus and of his contemporaries' rhetoric. *The Battle of the Books* is another example of Swift having fun at the expense of newspapers and journalists and their attempts to engage with contemporary history. Here he mocks the inadequacies of inappropriate ancient models of analysis as well as contemporary thinking.

In order to invoke the moral dimension of contemporary historical and political debates Swift takes, as his starting point, one of the multiplicity of maxims that his education and his contemporary intellectual climate offered. Through this use of maxims Swift highlighted the moral shortcomings of contemporary historical arguments. Current political concerns could be taken back to a supposedly innocent, underlying maxim, part of the repertoire of formulæ of political and moral philosophy. Other starting points were contemporary political pronouncements or the ideological assumptions that underpinned contemporary attitudes. For example, the basic premise of equality of all subjects of the realm of the United Kingdom involved in the Act of Union is employed successfully as the basis for the dissent encoded by Swift in *The Drapier's Letters*.

These are invoked only to be satirised. Swift's writing can devour any maxim in a wave of details, false trails and earnest argument that gradually gives way to chaos. Beginning with a seeming embrace, his writing eventually subverts the very orthodoxies he allegedly champions. The end result is often a degree of clarity and a new conviction of the distance between a current political situation and its alleged moral justification. *A Modest Proposal*, Swift's most outspoken and most audacious political work, (wherein he suggests that the hungry Irish

Swift's writing can ¶

Beginning with a seeming embrace,

devour any maxim ¶

his writing eventually subverts

in a wave of details, ¶

the very orthodoxies he allegedly champions.

false trails ¶

The end result is often a degree of clarity and a new conviction

and earnest argument ¶

of the distance between a current political situation

that gradually ¶

and its alleged moral justification.

gives way to chaos. #

peasantry should eat their children) is based on a seemingly innocent maxim - the assertion made by Temple in his *Essay upon the Advancement of Trade in Ireland* (1673) that 'the true and natural ground of trade and riches is, number of people in proportion to the compass of the ground they inhabit...' Swift included the abbreviated form of this maxim in his later publication of 1765, *Maxims Controlled in Ireland*, the penultimate entry of which is 'that people are the riches of a nation'. In *A Modest Proposal* Swift takes this idea – that the Irish poor should eat their own children - to its seemingly logical conclusion – one that renders it wholly unpalatable and immoral. Likewise, the power at the heart of *The Drapier's Letters* lies in Swift's returning to the English the maxim of equality of all subjects of the realm, and the maxim of the loyalty of all subjects and their duty to protect this realm - one he invokes both to avoid the charge of treason and to defeat the dreaded Wood's halfpence, the debased coinage destined, in his mind, to bankrupt the country. (In 1724 an English businessman, Wood was granted a patent to provide new copper coins for Ireland at an enormous personal profit but posing a serious threat to the nation's gold and silver reserves. Through *The Drapier's Letters*, published anonymously, Swift mobilised a powerful opposition in Ireland and the plan was dropped.)

The employment of the maxim as a starting point of investigation and analysis is the central literary strategy in all of Swift's Anglo-Irish classics. Around it he builds a series of clever assaults leading to a gradual disintegration of good sense, all delivered in an energetic prose, 'alive and breathing' as he felt history and morality should be, always aware of the social complexities of discourse, patently enjoying the discontinuities and the anarchy he was creating in the process. While some of his English readers believed *A Modest Proposal* to be sincere (a fact that amused Swift and confirmed his worst suspicions, as it were) this remains an illuminating satire which owes its success to Swift's inventive literary skills.

The contradictions and ambivalences of S
political allegiances but are there also in c
of Ireland clergyman of rank Swift's writ
and often included scatological material.
Swift on issues of his own moral conduct
companion Stella (Esther Johnson) and I
Homrigh). He is a writer for whom man
admiring his passion and his power of la
and his class prejudices. None, however, c
important influence on his successors.

ift's personality are not confined to his

er aspects of his profile. As a Church

could be considered blasphemous

veral of his biographers have indicted

relation to the women in his life, his

alleged mistress, Vanessa (Esther Van

eaders retain an ambivalent attitude,

uage while despairing of his misogyny

ibt his power as a satirist, nor his

The neglect of Ireland's people and economy and the decline in Ireland's fortunes that so troubled Swift continued into the next century. Maria Edgeworth shared Swift's distain for the English landlords who lived off the rents from their Irish estates while ignoring their civic responsibilities to their tenants and their communities. Although the Edgeworth family had been part of the Anglo-Irish ruling class since 1583, they were cultured and liberal-minded supporters of Enlightenment thinking and deplored the decline in Ireland they had witnessed over several generations. In 1800 Maria Edgeworth published *Castle Rackrent*, (set in 1782, written in the 1790s), a biting satirical work ostensibly lamenting the end of 'a long tradition', a phase of civilisation ending with the imminent Act of Union (1800). Edgeworth's novel, in fact, denounces the class who presided over this decline as well as the political orthodoxies that allowed this to occur and *Castle Rackrent* offered English readers an important insight into the reality of the situation in Ireland.

Within the text the Castle Rackrent of the title is nothing more than a pretentious hovel and the 'long tradition' it purports to lament, it transpires, is a mere eighteen years in duration. In true Swiftian style Edgeworth's novel ironically presents itself as a tribute, which effectively functions as an indictment of the ruling class in Ireland. Here she ostensibly offers the history of the Rackrent family narrated by their old retainer, a member of the native Irish, 'honest Thady' Quirk. He is both simple and gullible and displays no political allegiance or bitterness but is a form of stage-Irish fool whose comments are innocently delivered, but prove to be enormously revealing. He relates the hapless lives and untimely deaths of a series of masters he has served, all of whom he has outlived; Sir Patrick, Sir Murtagh, Sir Kit and Sir Conty Rackrent. At the close of the novel he is awaiting the acquisition of the estate by his own son, Jason Thady, a representative figure for the emergent Irish middle class, feared by Edgeworth and, as history attests, not scheduled to improve matters much for the general population.

Edgeworth's decision to fictionalise Ireland's plight is due to her recognition of Swift's literary strategy of the maxim taken to breaking point as a means of exposing the corruption at the heart of the matter. In *Castle Rackrent* we find the maxim of 'the noble family' and their 'time-honoured roles' as central to her indictment. The assumption that the former will honour the latter in the just management of their estates and tenants is exposed as absent, no longer the case in Ireland. These are the assumptions underpinning the feudal system of colonial rule, their absence in reality now responsible for the alarming decline in Ireland's situation in the late eighteenth and early nineteenth century. While in the novel it is the native Thady who assumes these to apply, it is very soon clear that no notion of a feudal relationship of reciprocal responsibilities ever enters the heads of the wastrel lords.

Edgeworth chronicles the demise of this clan through five generations of libertine, feckless, alcoholic and addictive fools and in fact gives us a *conte*, or short philosophical disputation designed to be instructive, on the failure of the idea of the moral family and its honourable role. Edgworth embraces the Swiftian doubleness in the addition to her main narrative of an extensive series of allegedly scholarly footnotes. These too have their Swiftian edge insofar as they are parodic and, in bold satire heighten the cultural, social and moral differences between the races. While the main narrative illustrates the customs and habits of Anglo-Irish lords, these footnotes ostensibly aim for a parity of values between the races (enshrined in the new Act of Union) by explaining native Irish traditions to the English.

The Swiftian reverse anthropology practised by Edgeworth can be found later in the writing of George Bernard Shaw. Born in 1856 he was educated in Dublin but moved to London in the 1870s to pursue a career as a dramatist. Like Swift, Shaw experienced a sense of apartness, an awareness of his own cultural hybridity and, like Swift, he developed a reputation as an outspoken, eccentric outsider in both countries. As a dramatist and as a writer Shaw was concerned to educate his readers and audiences to abandon their received opinions, their preconceived ideas of the world and of themselves. He was attracted to anarchism, and like Swift, he recognised how states could exploit, if not enslave, the poor and his writing constitutes a sustained attack on inherited opinions via humour and satire. Shaw's fundamental belief was one he shared with Swift, that is, that hypocritical moral codes were an impediment to the individual and thus to the economy. He extended his analysis to gender roles and here too tradition and outdated 'morality' were pronounced amoral as in *Mrs Warren's Profession* (1893), *Arms and The Man* (1894), and many other works are predicated on the Swiftian approach of sustained examination of an original maxim or set of so-called moral beliefs.

While Swift shied away from examinations of the individual self, Shaw's writing uses Swift's method to alert his audiences to the trends in self-deception that handicap us as individuals. As Declan Kiberd remarks, in what is itself a very Swiftian comment: "The Victorians harped so incessantly on notions of gentility as to throw serious doubt on their achievement of it" and Shaw, recognising this, lampooned his society's obsessions in many works where he plays off the archaic against the new, the traditional views on respectability and the more modern ideas of equality. He too offers extreme scenarios in his dramas and in his political writing, often aiming for the operatic and the absurd in an attempt to jolt his audiences and readers into recognition. He deplored much of what had occurred in Ireland and like Swift, he saw history and morality as incontrovertibly linked. As a socialist he railed against the exploitation of the masses and the hypocrisy of the ruling elite. Like Swift, he believed that the human subject was similar in key respects regardless of whatever culture he or she was raised in. He employed his predecessor's literary strategy of using the text to examine a central maxim. This is at the heart of one of Shaw's most successful plays, *John Bull's Other Island* (1904) where he challenges ideas of racial identity and racial stereotyping.

Many of his plays begin from this central strategy working through the dialogue and action to challenge the certainty and the humbug that underpins a great deal of moral complacency. Shaw's writing was acclaimed in his lifetime and his wit and cleverness was celebrated. However, many English audiences and readers were unthinkingly enamoured of the superficial charm of his comedy, failing to recognise their own society's shortcomings in the characters and action as he intended. In Ireland his reception was more favourable insofar as his political analysis, both in his writing and his drama, was embraced by many eager for social change.

However the satirical content was perceived, or not, the use of puns and other word games was a feature of Swift's writing (and is at the centre of the 'Jack Tales' already mentioned) and this is an aspect of Swift's legacy that Shaw also emulated to great effect. The value Swift put on an energetic use of language, on the passionate disavowal of that which offends and the fiery invective he is renowned for – much of this comes from his close proximity to the language of his neighbours in Dublin's Liberties, the area adjacent to St. Patrick's Cathedral. The Hiberno-English of these Dubliners often embraces a playful relationship to language, and to use a term invented by Joyce, a 'jocoserious' relationship to language. Joyce's *Ulysses* (1922) and his later masterpiece, *Finnegans Wake* (1939) takes this aspect of Swift's technique to extremes although it could be argued that the extent of Joyce's explorations and his distinct and richly encoded example of inventive wordplay has made this entirely his own. The scatological element of Swift's *œuvre* is also developed by Joyce and given a wealth of reference and richness of meaning surpassing his predecessor.

A truly pronounced presence of Swiftian literary strategies and techniques can be found in the works of the later writer, Brian O'Nolan or Flann O'Brien, where the influence of Swift is patently apparent. His writing has often been compared to that of James Joyce but his true literary precursor is Swift. In O'Brien's writing we find an embrace of Swiftian strategies unparalleled by another writer before or since. O'Brien wrote under a series of pseudonyms and his collected works include novels, plays, extensive journalism, essays, epigrams and television scripts. He, like Edgeworth, Shaw and Joyce enjoyed an ambivalent relationship with Irish culture and with his compatriots.

He was born in Strabane in 1911 and was initially educated at home in an Irish-speaking household, only attending school at the age of twelve when his family relocated to Dublin. He remained throughout his life a passionate supporter of the Irish language and his M.A. from University College Dublin was a study and translation of Middle-Irish poetry. On graduating in 1937 he began his career as a Civil Servant in the Department of 'Yokel Government', as he called it. His working life was spent simultaneously writing a daily column for *The Irish Times* under the pseudonym of Myles na gCopaleen. This ran for twenty five years, was hugely popular, enormously varied, topical and erudite and often very funny. No element of society escaped his criticism, his satirical wit and invective. He continued the mock philosophical dialogue – the satirical debunking of maxims, to wonderful effect with his frequent epigrams on Marx and Engels, Keats and Chapman, adapting the Swiftian method in a lighthearted fashion and following his predecessor's penchant for word games and puns. All of O'Brien's writing is Swiftian. He is Swift incarnate – Swift with a slightly more urbane, modernised consciousness. It is almost as if Swift himself were re-incarnated, equipped now with a full knowledge of Gælic culture, with the Irish language, and well acquainted with all the developments of modern life and the history of the intervening years.

Post-independence Ireland would seem to make redundant the motivations for hard hitting political satire but, for O'Brien, this was not the case as he astutely recognised that one set of determinants and controlling principles had merely replaced another. The Irish Free State and, later, the Irish Republic was, for O'Brien caught in the grip of a repressive fever of nationalistic piety to the extent that individual freedoms were again threatened. Cultural nationalism,

...the·use·of·puns¶

The value Swift put on an energetic use of language,

and·other·word·games¶

on the passionate disavowal of that which offends and the fiery invective he is renowned for –

was·a·feature¶

much of this comes from his close proximity to the language of his neighbours in Dublin's Liberties,

of·Swift's·writing...#

the area adjacent to St. Patrick's Cathedral.

Catholic evangelism, the cult of respectability, the championing of the Irish language (of which he was a true scholar and supporter) and most of all, the romanticising of the Irish rural poor - all of these had reached obsessive levels in the late 1930s and worked against the freedoms so hard won through revolution and civil war.

O'Brien's novels written in the late 1930s and early 1940s highlight the problems that this paradox produced for Irish people and his talent for Swiftian satire is truly apparent in their comic elements, their pseudo-seriousness and in their examination of first principles of delusional creeds – and especially in their scathing attacks on the status quo.

Swift had earlier referred to 'The Good People of Ireland', the innocent victims of colonial mis-rule. O'Brien adapted this and his work is both addressed to and critical of 'The Plain People of Ireland' who, in his satirical works are the essence of non-thinking conformity. His journalism frequently addresses this community and they feature also as characters in his most brilliant work, his first novel *At Swim Two Birds* (1939), a satirical masterpiece.

Critics have debated over this text for some time now but what can be established without doubt is the author's satirical intent and the work's multi-generic character. O'Brien takes a variety of literary forms including myth, legend, folklore, scientific treatises and a variety of modern literary genres, including the coming of age novel and the cowboy tale, much beloved of Irish readers at the time of writing. The unifying thread is the novel's central narrative constructed in the style of 'learned wit' championed by both Swift and Sterne. Here O'Brien gestures towards Swift's earlier writing in both tone and in the dominance of the narrator's own attempts at writing within the convention of the learned commentator - the ostensibly educated and sophisticated speaker drawing on established sources of ancient learning and applying them now to his current situation.

The result is high farce and much humour but O'Brien's intent is serious. Irish identity has been hijacked and has been moulded to a certain politicised script – that of the earnest nationalist ideal of pietistic peasants and pedantic believers in the myth of a romanticised, rural Irish race. This is effected through an unexamined embrace of all the clichés of Irish identity embodied in mythology, legend and more recent revivalists' narratives. O'Brien has found in Swift's writing a means of exposing the fallacy of subscription to these through exposing them – through taking the maxims of the cultural revivalists creeds and exposing the absurdity of their current application. The artistic renaissance that accompanied the movement to independence was, for O'Brien, now over, its energies gone, hijacked by more trivial and absurd preoccupations and repressive authorities eager to enforce limitations on creative enterprises that did not fit their narrow nationalistic ideals.

An Béal Bocht or *The Poor Mouth* (1941) is an attack on the revivalist ethos in both political and cultural matters that idealised rural peasant life as the essential Irish life, thus failing to attend to the economic depravation of a large section of the population. It also traces a continuum of misrepresentation of the Irish from the Victorian stage Irishman, through to the current stage Gæl and the obsessive adoption of Gælic identities now being promoted. The grinding poverty of the rural Irish had left them with no sense of identity, let alone any possibility of embracing a legendary and heroic affiliation with Cúchulainn or other ancient Gæls promoted at the time by the revivalists as models for contemporary manhood. With their identity continually hijacked over generations and now with their own willingness to adopt and adapt to the recent Gælic profile the Irish population were willing participants in their own tragedy.

This great satiric work relates the tale of the hapless O'Coonassa family and especially the elder son of the household, initially named Bonaparte but renamed Jams O'Donnell by the English schoolmaster who also renames all children in this way. Bonaparte's family live in dire poverty in Corch Dorcha, sharing their hovel with their animals and even registering a litter of piglets as children of the household. In line with Gulliver and *his* descent into madness in his reverence for horses over humans, this community cannot distinguish between humans and animals, mistaking the old, stinking pig, Ambrose, for an elder of their tribe. There is much hilarity in the tale but behind its moments of high farce O'Brien, like Swift, offers a true tragedy. He exposes the truth behind the rhetoric of rural glamorisation but also in this focus on animals he takes the first principle of the former imposed English identity for the Irish and demonstrates its aptness now in the impoverished conditions Ireland's own government and self-serving image-makers impose.

Throughout the novel O'Brien operates to the Swiftian formula again taking the English metaphor for the Irish peasant – the common image of the Irish with their pigs and later with simian connections – he takes these insulting metaphors, adds now the attributes of the more recent stage Gæl, and in the novel he raises the inevitable question of the Irish person's humanity. One of his characters, Sitric (named after the Viking hero, again echoing the aspirations of the community that seem absurd in their conditions) eventually prefers to live as an animal and departs for a life underwater as a seal. Depicting the Irish as compelled to live in the material and spiritual poverty that he outlines O'Brien equals the satiric quality of Swift's *A Modest Proposal* in the bleakness of the vision he offers. Through Swift's methods he offers powerful insights into the tragic situation that again the Irish were facing, proving himself a worthy successor to Swift in his capacity for hard-hitting satire.

Without Swift's example and his talent as a precursor of literary strategies for accurate and insightful exposure the literary encoding of the continuing travails of Irish society would not have been possible. Swift gave to subsequent generations of writers a sophisticated model for political satire that was inventive, insightful and above all effective and the Anglo-Irish literary tradition remains in the debt of this unlikely if not heroic exemplar.

Read more ...

Terry Eagleton, *The English Novel: an introduction*, Oxford, Blackwell Publishing, 2005.
Victoria Glendinning, *Jonathan Swift*, London, Pimlico, 1999.
Declan Kiberd, *Inventing Ireland: the literature of the modern nation*, London, Vintage Press, 1996.
Declan Kinerd, *Irish Classics*, London, Granta Books, 2001.
Sybil le Brocquy, *Swift's Most Valuable Friend*, Dublin, The Dolmen Press, 1968.
Angus Ross and David Woolley. *Jonathan Swift: a critical edition of the major works*, Oxford, Oxford University Press, 1984.

Notes on contributors

Andrew Carpenter
Andrew Carpenter, who is Professor of English at University College Dublin, was educated at Oxford and at UCD. His main research interest is in Swift and his contemporaries, and his two most recent books are anthologies entitled *Verse in English from Tudor and Stuart Ireland* (2003) and *Verse in English from Eighteenth-Century Ireland* (1998). He was until recently Head of the UCD School of English, Drama and Film, and is currently senior vice-president of the International Society for Eighteenth-Century Studies.

Valerie Coghlan
Valerie Coghlan is Librarian at the Church of Ireland College of Education, Dublin, where she also lectures on children's literature and visual literacy. She lectures on postgraduate courses at St. Patrick's College, Drumcondra, Dublin, and at University College Dublin. With Siobhán Parkinson she co-edits *Bookbird: an International Journal of Children's Literature* and is a former review editor of *Inis: the Children's Books Ireland Magazine*. She has co-edited several critical works about children's literature and is active in children's literature organisations in Ireland and overseas.

Eibhlín Evans
Eibhlín Evans grew up in Dublin before moving to England where she gained a PhD in English and Philosophy. She taught in universities there for many years before returning to Dublin in 2004. Since then she has been a member of the School of English and Drama at UCD. She has published academic articles, essays and reviews and has edited a collection of essays on Irish writing. She has also given talks, lectures and interviews on literary subjects and has been closely involved in the Dublin One City One Book initiative.

Celia Keenan

Celia Keenan is director of the MA Programme in children's literature, and a senior lecturer in English, at St. Patrick's College, Drumcondra. She is a member of the executive committee and former president and founding member of ISSCL, The Irish Society for the Study of Children's Literature. She co-edited *Studies in Children's Literature 1500-2000*, (Four Courts, 2004), and *Treasure Islands: studies in children's literature* (Four Courts, 2006), *The Big Guide to Irish Children's Books* (1996) and *The Big Guide 2: Irish children's books* (2000). She is a regular contributor to *INIS*.

Máire Kennedy

Máire Kennedy is Divisional Librarian with Dublin City Public Libraries in charge of Special Collections (early printed books and manuscripts). Her PhD in Book History is from UCD. She has published widely in Irish and international journals, and she is the author of *French Books in Eighteenth-Century Ireland* (Oxford, 2001). With Bernadette Cunningham, she edited *The Experience of Reading: Irish historical perspectives* (Dublin, 1999), and she has two chapters in *The History of the Irish Book*, volume III, *The Irish Book in English 1550-1800* (Oxford, 2005).

Ian Campbell Ross

Ian Campbell Ross is author of *Swift's Ireland* (1983) and co-editor of *Locating Swift* (1998), as well as having written a number of articles on Swift's life and work. His other works include *Public Virtue, Public Love: the early years of the Dublin Lying-in Hospital, the Rotunda* (1986), and *Laurence Sterne: a life* (2001). Aside from his work on the eighteenth century, he has also written *Umbria: a cultural history* (1995) and translated Gian Gaspare Napolitano's *To War with The Black Watch* (2007).

Mary Shine Thompson

Mary Shine Thompson is Dean of Research and Humanities at St. Patrick's College, Drumcondra. She is a founder member and current president of the Irish Society for the Study of Children's Literature (ISSCL), a board member of *Poetry Ireland*, and chair of the Bisto Book of the Year Award 2006-7. Recent books include *Divided Worlds: studies in children's literature*, (2007), co-edited with Valerie Coghlan; *Selected Plays by Austin Clarke* (2005); *Treasure Islands: studies in children's literature* (2005), and *Studies in Children's Literature* (2004), co-edited with Celia Keenan. She has written biographical notes of authors and story notes for the twenty *Irish Independent Great Children's Books* (2006).

Illustrations

First edition 1726
*Travels into Several Remote Nations
of the World. In four parts.
By Lemuel Gulliver, first a surgeon,
and then a captain of several ships*,
London, printed for Benj.
Motte, 1726.

Dublin edition 1727
*Travels into Several Remote
Nations of the World. In four parts.
By Lemuel Gulliver, first a surgeon,
and then a captain of several ships.
With Cuts and Maps of the Author's
Travels,* Dublin, printed for
G. Risk, G. Ewing, and W. Smith
in Dame-Street, 1727.

Edinburgh edition 1820s
*Gulliver's Travels into the Kingdoms
of Lilliput and Brobdingnag,*
embellished with neat engravings
on wood, Edinburgh, Oliver and
Boyd, [1820?].

Anonymous illustrator 1863
*Gulliver's Travels: a voyage
to Lilliput and Brobdingnag,*
by Jonathan Swift, London,
Longman, Green, Longman,
Roberts, and Green, 1863.

Anonymous illustrator [1890s]
Gulliver's Travels, a new edition
with many illustrations, London,
George Routledge and Sons,
[1890s].

F.M.B. Blaikie
Gulliver's Travels, told to the
children by John Lang, with
pictures by F.M.B. Blaikie,
London, T.C. and E.C. Jack, n.d.
[191-].

John Brooking
*The City of Dublin, 1728,
reproduced from A Map of the
City and Suburbs of Dublin by
Charles Brooking*, Dublin, Irish
Architectural Archive and The
Friends of the Library, Trinity
College, Dublin, 1983.

René Bull
Travels into Several Remote
Nations of the World, edited
by F.J. Harvey Darton, and
with illustrations by René Bull,
London, Wells Gardner, Darton
and Co., Ltd., [1940s].

Drapier's Letter 1724
Jonathan Swift, *A Letter to the
Whole People of Ireland, by M. B.
Drapier*, Dublin, printed by John
Harding, [1724].

J.J. Grandville
Gulliver's Travels, Jonathan
Swift, with the illustrations of
J. J. Grandville, new foreword
by Denis Donoghue, New York,
Da Capo, 1988. (Illustrations
commissioned for a French
translation in 1838).

John Hassall
Gulliver's Travels, retold for little
folk by Agnes Grozier Herbertson,
illustrated by John Hassall, R.I.,
London, Blackie and Son Limited,
[1915].

A.E. Jackson
Gulliver's Travels, adapted for the
young by W.B. Scott, illustrated by
Albert E. Jackson, London, Ernest
Nister, [1911].

P.J. Lynch
A Voyage to Brobdingnag, after an
original oil painting by P. J. Lynch
in Johnston Central Library,
Cavan.

Thomas Morten
*Gulliver's Travels into Several
Remote Regions of the World,
by Dean Swift*, a new edition,
illustrated by T. Morten, London,
Cassell, Petter and Galpin,
[1864-65].

R.G. Mossa
Gulliver's Travels, pictures by
R.G. Mossa, London, Hodder
and Stoughton, 1938.

Le Nouveau Gulliver
Pierre-Francois Guyot
Desfontaines, *Le nouveau Gulliver,
ou voyage de Jean Gulliver, fils du
capitaine Gulliver, traduit d'un
manuscrit anglois par Monsieur
L.D.F.*, Paris, chez la veuve
Clouzier, librarie, et Francois le
Breton, librarie, 1730.

Parliament House 1811
The Picture of Dublin for 1811,
Being a Description of the City...,
by John James M'Gregor, Dublin,
printed for the proprietor,
by J. and J. Carrick, 1811.

Willy Pogány
Gulliver's Travels, edited
by Padraic Colum, presented by
Willy Pogány, London, George
G. Harrap, 1919, and reprint 1937.

V.A. Poirson
Gulliver's Travels, with prefactory
memoir by George Saintsbury and
one hundred and eighty coloured
and sixty plain illustrations [by
V.Armand Poirson], London,
Nimmo, 1886.

Arthur Rackham
Gulliver's Travels, illustrated by
Arthur Rackham, Letchworth,
Temple Press, 1937, and reprint
1939.

Louis Rhead
Gulliver's Travels into Several
Remote Nations of the World by
Jonathan Swift (Lemuel Gulliver)...
with more than one hundred
illustrations by Louis Rhead, New
York and London, Harper and
Brothers Publishers, 1913.

Chris Riddell
Jonathan Swift's GULLIVER, retold
by Martin Jenkins, illustrated by
Chris Riddell, London, Walker,
2004.

Rocque Map 1756
John Rocque, *An Exact Survey*
of the City and Suburbs of Dublin,
London, John Rocque, 1756.

St. Patrick's 1828
The New Picture of Dublin, or
Stranger's Guide Through the Irish
Metropolis, Dublin, William Curry,
Jun. and Co., 1828.

Swift Bust
Volume XIV. Containing Letters
to and from Dr. Jonathan Swift,
Dublin, George Faulkner, 1767,
frontispiece.

Swift Hospital 1733
Jonathan Swift, *A Serious and*
Useful Scheme, to Make an Hospital
for Incurables, of Universal Benefit
to all His Majesty's Subjects, printed
at London, and, Dublin: printed
by George Faulkner, 1733.

Swift Portrait
Jonathan Swift, *The Works of*
Dr. J. Swift, D.S.P.D. in eleven
volumes, Dublin, George Faulkner,
1763, frontispiece portrait,
G. Vertue sculpt.

J.G. Thomson
Gulliver's Travels, illustrated with
upwards of 300 wood-engravings,
from designs by J.G. Thomson,
engraved by W.L. Thomas,
London, S.O. Beeton, 1864.

Voyages de Gulliver 1730
Jonathan Swift, *Voyages du capitaine Lemuel Gulliver, en divers pays eloignez*, A La Haye, chez Gerard Vander Pœl, 1730.

Voyages de Gulliver 1813
Voyages de Gulliver, traduits de l'anglais, de Swift, par l'abbe Des Fontaines, 4 volumes, Paris, Chez Genets Jeune, 1813.

Acknowledgements

Edited by Máire Kennedy and Alastair Smeaton
Illustrations from the collections of Dublin City Public Libraries

Dublin City Public Libraries acknowledges permissions granted
to reproduce illustrations by the following:

Charles Brooking: *A Map of the City and Suburbs of Dublin, 1728*,
by Charles Brooking. Courtesy of The Board of Trinity College Dublin

P.J. Lynch: *A Voyage to Brobdingnag*, after an original oil painting by P.J. Lynch
in Johnston Central Library, Cavan. www.pjlynchgallery.com

Willy Pogány: Reproduced by kind permission of Chambers Harrap
Publishers, Ltd.

Arthur Rackham: Arthur Rackham / Mary Evans Picture Library
www.maryevans.com

Chris Riddell: Illustrations © 2004 Chris Riddell from GULLIVER
retold by Martin Jenkins & illustrated by Chris Riddell.
Used by permission of Walker Books Ltd, London SE11 5HJ

Every effort has been made to trace copyright holders and to obtain their
permission for the use of copyright material. The publisher apologises for
any errors or omissions in the above list and would be grateful if notified
of any corrections that should be incorporated in future reprints or editions
of this book.